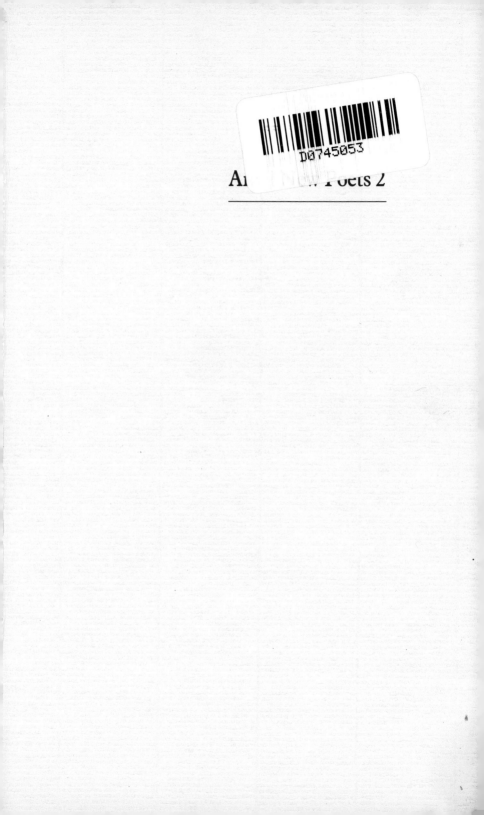

An            Poets 2

# Anvil New Poets 2

*Edited by Carol Ann Duffy*

Anvil Press Poetry

Published in 1995
by Anvil Press Poetry
69 King George Street London SE10 8PX

This book is published
with financial assistance
from The Arts Council of England

ISBN 0 85646 262 4

Designed and composed by Anvil
Photoset in Plantin by Typestream
Printed at Alden Press Limited
Oxford and Northampton
Great Britain
Distributed by Password, Manchester

A catalogue record for this book
is available from the British Library

# Contents

# Introduction

HERE ARE NINE new poets I wish to commend to the reader. Their ages range from 24 to 50 and, although some share clear affinities with each other and some are quite different, they all, in my view, possess an honest and distinct poetic energy. Some of the poets here have attended the inestimably valuable courses run by the Arvon Foundation; some have received time-buying Eric Gregory awards; some have published their own pamphlets or broadsheets and sold them at readings. Anvil Press offers this anthology as a showcase for the talents of these new poets, none of whom has yet published a collection.

Sean Boustead is 25 and first began to write poetry during 'a knockabout Salford childhood'. Salford has given him a good ear, apparent in all the poems here and he feels more comfortable acknowledging the influence of pop music than of Eng. Lit. The poem 'Pop Pop' combines his skills well. That said, he has a natural lyricism which seems to be becoming more assertive. His work can both startle and entertain.

Colette Bryce was born in Northern Ireland in 1970 and, like Boustead, is a writer to whom place is important in terms of the way people speak. She is comfortable with the dramatic monologue, with trying to net the small, memorable dramas of a life. Her concern for an accessible language, a language interested in communication, is evident, although form is clearly also an attraction. She can write effortlessly of what it is to be young and to leave home behind.

Like Bryce, Kate Clanchy has written a poem concerning the tragic murder, in 1993, of James Bulger. She differs from Bryce and from Boustead, however, in writing out of a much more obvious literary tradition. Larkin is an identifiable influence, not least in her ability to *end* a poem effectively. Clanchy has a distinct and, for me, completely fresh way of writing about the relations between men and women. She writes with a sense of excitement or loss which is memorable.

Oliver Comins writes an affirmative, open poetry which has its source emphatically in the writer's life. His themes are the people of childhood, holidays, beer and cricket, characters encountered through work and travel. His poems have grace and truth. They can be read and re-read with a deepening pleasure, particularly the sequence after a painting by Frank Batson, 'Playing Out Time in an Awkward Light'.

Christina Dunhill's poems take risks, are sexy, bursting with vivid images, as in the poem 'Old People'. The raunchy 'The Shape of Her' is one of the best lesbian love poems I've read in recent years. And her work, like that of many of the poets here, is no stranger to humour ('Old People' again and 'Andrew Hardie's Girls and Boys').

Alice Oswald's poetry possesses a startling originality. She has doubtless read Herbert, Hopkins and Hughes, but there is something new here. Her subjects, the things themselves, be they birds, weather, or plants, are present in a thrilling way in both the language and the forms of her poems. Some of her lines seem inspired and yet only an insistence on crafting could have produced the end results.

Richard Price, despite his well-known rôle as a poetry magazine editor in Scotland and, latterly, in England, retains an individual voice in which intense feelings of love, or dislocation, are packed into often short, complex lyrics. There is a tension in reading his poems which is created by his care for words, by the integrity of his distillation.

Like Price, Mike Venner has a strong, though different, political edge. Of all the poets here, he is the most rooted in performance and his poems have the ability to perform *on* the page. Venner is concerned with song, with the speakable. But words for him are also a way of making 'new sense'. He is an angry, high-energy, audible poet and he knows how to use these qualities. Some of his poems made me laugh out loud.

John Whale, like Ian Duhig, with whom he shares some common ground, lives in Leeds. Whale makes childhood strange and mythical. He is obsessed with the oddness of words – 'cephalopoda', 'curare', 'simoon', 'gorgettes' – and combines hyperbole and erudition in poems which plunder science and history to form their sparkling entertainments. A fascination with human behaviour informs his work.

These nine new poets are serious about language and they are enjoying language. They are clearly aware, not least as readers, of the varied, warm and bustling life of contemporary poetry and they are assured enough to become a part of it and to add to it. I am very happy to introduce their work here.

CAROL ANN DUFFY

*London, October 1994*

# SEAN BOUSTEAD

# Heroes

They were angry and they were our heroes,
far away, in our childhood, brittle daisies
straining out of kerb-cracks on the long roads.
Even if they died of overdoses,
our heroes, we called them queer clean angels,
we scratched their lyrics into black textbooks
amongst the verbs and difficult angles.
We wore the heroes' clothes, we kicked and fucked
and for a while anger was our fashion,
anger, as if we might become heroes
through a kind of emotional fission.
Down the chip-shop roads, down the long dark roads,
we sang what they sang and could taste our lives
and we kicked small stones along yellow lines.

## Pop Pop

Hey, smash the glass, the glass has shown you thin,
it shows your hair stringy, it shows your skin
pale and plain-chocolate-sickly and that's it.
It means nothing, what the glass says means shit.
    Break it,
throw your old school papers in the dustbin,

pick up the remote control and hit play.
Just let it happen. Turn, turn in such a way
that it seems the world is turning for you,
    press into
your parents' bedroom, slip into the loo.
Hey, the weather's crap and it's a Sunday.

Hey, you're starting work soon, somehow your hands
are heavier, they have the feel of England's
    summers,
idle, undramatic. Can you catch the drummer?
how he holds off, he slows it, to a dreamer's
movement. O, and can you catch the whole band?

it means you, simply, and the aches and bruises
    this song leaves are
what will one day prove that you were younger,
what you'll still dream of, when you feel no longer
the dull insistence of your breasts and fingers.
O, read, or try to catch what the news says:

    *colder,*
*some sunshine.* Maybe play the song back, louder,
but sit still. Do you feel that taut pressure?
O, my poor baby, do you have a wish for
high silent mountains, O, where you could smash your
Mickey Mouse wristwatch against the dumb boulders?

# Institutions

They were funny and had a funny name
and after school we played them, played their moods,
and I always played the quiet one. Moon,
their name was, such a strange and fine name
it made me think of the faint trace of hooves
in the moon's dust. One was always silent,
and when he spoke we thought him insolent
as if his words touched life, all life was moved
like a guilty congregation, silent.
But it was his brother who turned violent,
his brother who was locked up here, smiling.
See the Moon, we laugh, the Moon is shining,
see in the sky the Moon is pressing on.
I was brought in with minor depression.

## The Man with the Blue Face

This is the man with the blue face, moving
down the dirt backing where the schoolchildren
pick at their dark uniforms, strike matches.
This is the young man with the sad blue face,
the man whose body failed, who saw one day
the old lady gripping library books
and watching him, watching as his body
drifted off into the slow shopping crowd,
drifted into what she called the winter's hurt.
This is the thin and difficult blue man
asking the schoolchildren for their last match.
Look – in the vaguest of winds the match fails.

# Advice

Surround with high walls whoever you dream yourself to be.
Then, in the bits of the garden you might happen to see
through bars on the gate,
plant only the flowers that seem to you the most gay
so that you're believed to be like this.
Where nobody will ever come, plant nothing.

Make flowerbeds like those that other people have
in the parts of the garden other people catch a glimpse of –
make flowerbeds as if you were going to show them.
Where you are yourself, where nobody will ever see them,
let the flowers coming through the ground live,
let natural grasses thrive.

Be circumspect, guarded.
Let other people see a garden
and nothing more of what you are –
tended, taken care
of – maybe the occasional native flower brushing
up against grass so poor not even you can see it . . .

*(Translated from Fernando Pessoa)*

## Bob Turner and His Wife

Marriage, natural enough, yet strange, like snow
    over England's modest April, cold
to wake to, took place. Numerous photos:

    they seem happy, they
hold hands, they grin – stiffly – for some reason
    seeming pantomimic in those old

styles. Maybe you could say all fashion
    changes; even the street-names
synonymous with any Southport-half-day passion

    they found changed. In time
she waved the five children into school,
    he brought the bacon home,

they contemplated TV sets like holes
    having to be exact if
something is to grow. His heart failed,

    but he had been sick
quite a fair while. And rain cracked,
    on paving-stones, on bricks,

and pretty girl-guides flitted round stacked
    rubbish, up steps. The widow
thought she could feel eyes against her back,

    thought she saw him. Snow
came: delicate, isolate snow. And it seemed
    there'd never been such snow,

it had never snowed before, it seemed.
    On the shining emptied streets
it had never snowed before, it seemed.

# The Good Times

I have worn my politics to parties
but been framed at strip-jack-naked.
Later, still nude, I've turned the music
down, I've strained to hear bedroom doors
pushed shut, precisely. I have staggered home,
underpants on backwards, someone else's socks. Stopped
in poor districts, I have made piss
carry on the wind. I have proved
an inexpensive beauty. Like evil, I survive.

# A Landscape After War

There is peace in a landscape after war.
Flowers, tourists, lean around the walls
to which the poet, who was paid to shout
but shouted incorrectly, was led to, shot;
seven of the trees in the old pictures
lean indifferently; beautiful vultures
move through the air in beautiful circles
while young soldiers pass on scratched bicycles.
It is a gracious and deserved reward,
the peace in a landscape, after the war,
the spring released, readjusting, as if
war after all is made by those who live –
spring is a difficult inheritance
only the children take to be a chance,
children gathering in flowers at the wall
or playing a particular general
while old women struggle white stones across
makeshift vegetable patches and curse.
This is how war must be recovered from –
usually with mild tablets, and with time,
and letting nothing much happen: stories
mistranslated in the bars by tourists;
someone fixing a loose tile; from a torn
dark case a doctor taking out a guitar.

# Walls

He said it was a kind of emptiness,
like faint memories. He said there were holes
in his life, there was violence on the news,
and it would be nice and healthy, he hoped,

and at that time it was fashionable,
and all the first month there was easy wind.
Then he found one dead, behind the stables,
kneeling. Dying is hard to understand,

and every day he seemed to take in less –
the public warning at the farm-entrance,
suddenly the young men in city-dress.
I thought it seemed to him a kind of dance,

a kind of aisle, improvised, and the sheep
shuffling down the aisle like church-hall foxtrot
friends, though what they found there was not friendship.
He died at each of the thirty seven shots,

I thought that I saw each of the shots fold
into him. He hated speaking on the phone;
when I rang he was out somewhere in the fields,
tapping at the perfect walls around the fields.

## Young Mothers

They gather into chance conspiracies, young mothers,
at the doctor's or the dole-place.
They have serious and careful eyes but
chat advert words, the user-friendly language
of a tabloid, of a latest craze.
Somehow I do not smile to them,
young mothers, they have guessed men correctly,
their minds seem kept exact and lighted
like a secret military library. Their prams
seem to push the memory of when
they became changed, these women, push something
that was not fighting an especial war
or following careers, none of the reasons
men believe. They move as if caught
dancing on after a record's end. Their
pram-wheels catch on the pavement cracks.

# Gents

*for Ian*

It is a game I play – pacing
up and down in public toilets,
sneaking looks at the men pissing.
Spare me your disgrace – tell it

to the loveless and the obscene.
Since I am shy and quite genteel
mine is more a name than a sin.
I like most men who are gentle –

I shall plead gentleness and hurt
if ever I am seen and caught.
To hold in evidence my heart
It must be a packed and hushed court.

## Easy Listening

A song's desperate, hard
sound on car-radios,
in locked back-yards,
out of bedroom windows –
he loved the harder songs
when he was very young,

up late, in her small room.
(Well, he was free to dream.)
Once she said the words
emptied her, like wards
looking out to slate-roofs
that were grey and rain-damp –

O, for Christ's sake!
it was only pop music,
only a kind of wishing:
for microwaves and sliced loaves,
for beauty and wisdom,
for important love.

# Leaving

After seven years of
day-dreaming of sailing
always somewhere far off,
after stealing
fantasies about
girls stood around

the shopping-front
in school-uniforms,
girls carving an affront
into the one form
still intact and left –
not long after this, he left.

And things happened:
the curious book-
store opened;
in the brook
a vicar drowned
who'd only been down

two days from the country.
It seemed death had held
back, had been counting
on his leaving to help.
It seemed death was a lover
listening for his engine turning over.

# COLETTE BRYCE

# Woman & Turkey

I needed a drink before handling it,
the clammy skin, thin and raw.
I remembered touching a dead Bishop once;
Sign of the Cross, shivers.

Its feet, ditched in the sink, reached
like withered hands appealing.
The crack of its bones chilled my own.
I sank another, severed the neck.

The membranous eyes were unsettling,
the shrunken head bereft on the block,
the clutch and the squelch as innards slopped out –
gizzard, heart, lungs; stillborn.

I finished the bottle to see it through
and caught the scene in the night behind glass,
a corpse like a glove to my wrist.
I am sick to the stomach of Christmas.

It's hazy then until Boxing Day.
A carcass in bits, picked clean. I wake
to blood trapped under my nails,
to the delicate snap of a wishbone.

# Emigrant

On the wet deck, as you watch the line
where sea becomes a threatening sky,
you're at vanishing point;

a place between ports,
where land fails on every side
so there's no telling forwards or backwards
any more, or if you care, or would
have it any different given the chance.

And you've left again the vanishing point
of not wanting to stay,
and not wanting to travel back
to where layers of distance
will shut like Russian dolls around your heart;

back to the vanishing point of the phone-calls,
the closing choke of coins, the tick
of the units diminishing fast, streets
resurfacing through glass, a voice
on the line full of absence, frangible, gone.

And harbour lights take form
like new constellations; and you miss
the deepening lines on your mother's face.

# Lines

I have given birth to a see-through child.
In the midwife's cloth its skin cools
and sets to a delicate shell, not quite
opaque but vague like frosted glass.

Closer, I see the insides press
like noses smudged on windows,
through a web of a million arteries
bleached with a notable absence of blood.

I don't know what to do with it.
I am trying to get back to my mother;
but the cab-driver drops it as I try to pay,
and all I can do is stand here and stare

at my broken baby, spilt across the kerb –
when my sister springs from a childhood game,
skipping towards me, laughing. *Calm down*,
she says, *it all fits back together, look. See?*

# Buster

Under a 40 watt bulb the plastic kettle bubbles
along to a scratched Patsy Cline. A swivel mirror
cranes its neck as if to catch the light, but finds
two redwebbed eyeballs, bugged in a stubbled face.
Buster braves his throat to the wavering blade.

Shaved, he scuttles the stairs and out
then labours back three flights with a bagful
of jangling bottles and packets of cigarettes.
Midnight, he shivers and thumps the fire,
whose single bar is growing dim, causing his jar

of 5p coins to suddenly shudder, suddenly ring.
Come 2.00, he roars a toast to the coats that hang
to a human shape on the back of his door.
And he was hoovering come 4.00, and weeping; just
cursing the ups and downs of the fuckin' floor.

# Boys Sitting on a Wall
# in Liverpool During the Trial

The wall exhibits three. Large,
average, small. Small's feet are flat
on the ground. He is resting his elbows
on his knees, he is resting his chin
in the heels of his hands. He is ageing.

Average is burning a candle,
dripping intricate patterns
on the pavement, sometimes on his skin.
His eyes wince as wax pales to curious
warts on his hands. He is worried

sick about things he can't understand.
Large is jumpy as a man
awaiting results of a cancer scan.
He is watching Average melting wax,
he is watching the digits on his watch.

The city is quiet as God.
There's been a killing here and the jury
is out. Nobody knows what it means.
The photographer offers a fiver apiece
for their picture. For ten, they agree.

# Itch

I believe that Jesus lives
deep in the ditch of my mother's ear,

an unreachable itch that never leaves;
and I believe when Jesus breathes

a million microscopic hairs
lean in the breeze like sapling trees.

Things I begin to tell her
I believe sometimes she cannot hear

for the whispering like wishes
of Jesus softly breathing there.

# Epilogue

The journey back was a nightmare.
Alice was menstrual, resentful,
complaining she *always* has to drive;
she was gripping the wheel at arms length
as though appalled, repelled,
as we ripped through a sprawled
and sleeping landscape into the sky.
She seemed to be lost in a half-trance
of remembering, when the car tensed –

and the white rabbit in Alice's eye
was a stark black stare in the fast lane,
pulped by a tyre on the passenger side
sending a shudder up through the bodywork.
I screamed, and Alice's knuckles gleamed
on the steering-wheel, bright with shock,
till we finally stopped so I could be sick
on the motorway roadside grass. *It was too late*,
Alice whispered, *We were going too fast*.

# Form

For some time I have been starving myself,
and not in the interest of fashion,
but because it is something to do
and I do it well. I'm writing this
as my only witness has been the glass
on the wall. Someone must know
what I've done and there's no one to tell.

Commitment is the main thing. After this,
the emptiness, the hunger isn't a sacrifice
but a tool. I found I was gifted, good.
And full of my vocation, sat or stood
at the mirror just watching my work
take shape, conform to my critical eye.

Or would lie, supine, stomach shrinking,
contracting, perfecting its concave line.
Each day gave a little more: depth
to the shallows of the temples, slight
depressions of the cheeks; contrast
to the clavicle, the ankle bone, the rib,
the flawless five-line verses of my feet.

But one night I dressed and went for a walk
and felt a latent contamination of eyes
from windows and cars. I'd been feeling
strange, somehow encased, the hollow rush
of my own breath like tides in the shell
of my own head. A woman passed

and I saw myself in her glance, her expression
blank as a future. The next day I woke
to double vision, everything suddenly
terribly clear only twinned. My hearing too,
was distracted. I sipped some water
and retched. My speech, when I test it,
has stretched to a distant slur like a voice

from behind a door. I would think
I was losing my mind if it wasn't behind
all this from the start. Tonight
there's an almost imperceptible buzzing
in my bones, like the sound of electric razors,
a lawn-mower several gardens down.

I worry that they're crumbling
under my skin, dissolving like aspirin.
I worry that my bones are caving in.
When I sit my joints begin to set.
I try to stand and I'm hit by a shift
in gravity. The point where an aircraft
lifts and enters flight. And I think

my sight is burning out. I think it is losing
its pupil heart. Objects are calmly vacating
their outlines, colours slowly absorbing the dark.
In my dream the shovels uncover a hare,
preserved in its form, its self-shaped lair,
and I'm travelling in. There is no going back.

## The Potential

All day at work my temples throbbed
as everyone yelled in voices lost to machinery
steadily blasting noise, then home where the infant
wailed as my wife pitched her voice above it,
filling me in, the TV blared its godawful din

and the washing machine screamed into Spin
so I slammed the kitchen door, but the boys
were playing apaches singing *WAH WAH WAH WAH WAH*
It was then that I felt the potential.
I went for a walk.

I'm walking. Tense. Taut as a wire poised
at a gulping throat. I picture someone's head
shrink back, the way the eyes would bulge.
An invisible weapon, tight round my fingers,
bites back flesh. Guitar string.

I imagine I'm giving someone a kicking,
boot in the guts, hard, again. Or gripping
a neck I'm punching the face, fast,
till I feel that I'm through.
Just lately I think about things I'd never do.

I walk this maze repetition of streets
but a tuning fork note persists and drills
in the place behind my eyes, on either side
a sweeping pulse on my eardrums
echoes the thump in my heart,

I walk. And now my fists
are stashed safe inside my jacket;
their nasty suggestions
strangle and drown in pocket-soft cloth.
My nails impaled in my palms, I walk, and walk.

## Wish You Were

Here, an aftertaste of traffic taints
the city's breath, as mornings
yawn and bare this street

like teeth. Here, airplanes leaving
Heathrow scare this house
to trembling; these rooms protect

their space with outstretched walls,
and wait. And evenings fall
like discs in a jukebox, playing

a song called *Here*, night after night.
*Wish you were.* Your postcards
land in my hall like meteorites.

## Wine

The corkscrew lifts its elegant arms
like the Pope greeting tourists
on his balcony. Tonight we drink

religiously. Fill to a shivering inch
of the brink, carefully, almost
warily. Tonight I drink to you,

and you to me, but this time,
seriously. As if following, word
for word in the clink, a ceremony.

# Young

Loose stacks of cassettes collapse
to the slam of the door behind us.
We take the stairs in twos and threes,
we don't know where
we might be
this time next year, but meanwhile,

we apply to the future in lunch-breaks;
taste the possibility,
the sweet adhesive strip of A4
envelopes on tongues,
punch the day, and run
to post, to home, and out.

We eye each other up
as future lovers; our faces smooth
as blank maps of undiscovered countries,
where only we might go.
We mean to go, we thumb the guides,
we spin the globe

and halt it at Calcutta, then Alaska,
now Japan, and plan. *Imagine.*
Not for us
the paper lanterns of remember,
but the hard bright bulbs
of sheer want.

We reminisce at length
about the future, which is better;
we harbour it in our hearts like a terrible crush.
We laugh, and drink to this in rented rooms.
We think *Not this,*
*but older, elsewhere, soon.*

# KATE CLANCHY

# Men

I like the simple sort, the soft white collared ones
smelling of wash that someone else has done,
of apples, hard new wood. I like the thin-skinned,
outdoor, crinkled kind, the athletes, big-limbed,
who stoop to hear, the moneyed men, the unironic
leisured sort who balk at jokes and have to blink,
the men with houses, kids in cars, who own
the earth and love it, know themselves at home
here, and so don't know they're born, or why
born is hard, but snatch life smack from the sky,
a cricket ball caught clean that fills the hand.
I put them all at sea. They peer at my dark land
as if through sun on dazzling waves and laugh.

## The Aerialist

Having finally dined with the aerialist,
I've found him just a college gymnast,
fresh pressed East Coast boy dismissed
from frosty Dartmouth February last,

distinguished just by his wish to kiss
the sleek striped roof of the circus tent, sniff
sugar mixed with sawdust, trodden grass, and seek
the chalky hand of the Only Candelabra Girl.

Let me lift my glass and drink to the quirk
that lets him fly, slick in tights and lycra,
nightly through the Gods. I shall crick my neck
to see him spin his new wife high above me

by a rope from teeth to nose, candles
in her fingers, candles in her toes.

## Can't Argue With It

These boys I teach wear gold like armour:
they hold up hardened hands of rings to flick
the shivering light like knives as they rock and kick.

They wear their names, short cold sounds,
on gold chains at their straining necks, and lock
bare arms on thin young chests and rock and kick

and draw thin breaths through narrow mouths.
I watch their feet, as they rock and kick, and hear
them breathe and ask them why, and what, and why.

# Tip

Get a hat, a homburg, keep
it on in bars, tipped
so just your profile shows.

Imply a smile, one-sided. Perhaps
a scar to hold it.
Seek out the half-light, stand

in it oblique, a silhouette. Smoke
a blue-edged trail
in icy air, by a lamp-post, let

your few sharp words intensify
to clouds. Be lean.
Be leaning on the bar I plan

to enter. Irony's the ice I keep
my dreams in. Drop
some in your whisky. Hold it there.

# Poem for a Man with No Sense of Smell

This is simply to inform you:

that the thickest line in the kink of my hand
smells like the feel of an old school desk,
the deep carved names worn sleek with sweat;

that beneath the spray of my expensive scent
my armpits sound a bass note strong
as the boom of a palm on a kettle drum;

that the wet flush of my fear is sharp
as the taste of an iron pipe, midwinter,
on a child's hot tongue; and that sometimes,

in a breeze, the delicate hairs on the nape
of my neck, just where you might bend
your head, might hesitate and brush your lips,

hold a scent frail and precise as a fleet
of tiny origami ships, just setting out to sea.

## Slattern

I leave myself about, slatternly,
bits of me, and times I liked:
I let them go on lying where
they fall, crumple, if they will.
I know fine how to make them walk
and breathe again. In private night
or on the train, I dream I'm dancing,
or lying in someone's arms who says
he loves my eyes in French, and again
and again I am walking up your road,
that first time, bidden and wanted,
the blossom on the trees, light,
light and buoyant. *Pull yourself
together*, they say, quite rightly, but
she is stubborn, that girl,
that hopeful one, still walking.

# Designs

Since the tragic death of your young wife
in that sudden conflagration of bush grass
on the curve of the coast road, since I attended
the closed coffin funeral in my netted hat,
sent the blotted tender letter you smoothed
with your square fingers to better feel
its understanding, since our holiday in Scotland
where you learned to love again, I have
applied myself to the plan of our dream house.

Our lounge, wide as the deck of a ship, runs
the length of the sea view terrace, done out
in terracotta with a border of Greek keys. The chairs
are laidback, Frank Lloyd Wright, accessories,
largely chrome. Outside, at present, are ponds
and prairie grass. I am calling to ask your opinion
on the position of the porch swing, and if those stands
of grass with their grand sweeps of dry clean blades
could, in some small way, distress you.

## Pathetic Fallacy

You can't get drenched, however much you wish it.
You could stand all autumn on our corner
stubborn as a lamp-post, and watch drains fill
and then spill over, puddles stretch to dimpled floods,
and still not feel the rain run through you,
cooling, cleaning out. Your skin's too tight to let it.

You could wait till all your clothes had shrunk
to sodden sails and both your shoes had split
and curled like flowers, hair slicked down to water-weeds
and eyebrows dripped clear stalactites
to tide pools in your eyes, but your heart
would go on pumping the same muddy blood around.

For rain is not relieving, nor new either.
It's our own old wet reused, gone acid,
coming down still muttering its boring song of loss.
It pisses down, it spits, it lands like sweat gone cold,
and when its fingers mock our necks, old hurts,
like scraps of paper, resurface in the drains.

# Timetable

We all remember school, of course:
the lino warming, shoe bag smell, expanse
of polished floor. It's where we learned
to wait: hot-cheeked in class, dreaming,
bored, for sour milk, for noisy now.
We learned to count, to rule off days,
and pattern time in coloured squares:
purple English, dark green Maths.

We hear the bells, sometimes,
for years, and heed the squeal
of white on black. We walk, don't run
in awkward pairs, hoping for the open door,
a foreign teacher, fire drill. And love's
long aertex summers, tennis sweat,
and somewhere, someone singing flat.
The art room, empty, full of light.

## Mitigation

We think you know the secret places,
the ones you called, perhaps, *Big Sands,*
*The Den,* or *Grassy Hill*. They loom up large
behind your eyes. Those hands that stroke
your signet ring were once, like ours, blunt-
fingered, small, and clutched at grass or clenched
a stone, and loved the tender, ticking throat

of panicked bird or retching child. You
watched the films. You played at Vlad.
That doll was yours whose head came off.
You stored her up behind the fort, the patch
of dirt around her mouth. There's something
buried in the park, a shallow grave, a rotting
thrush. You know the place. And know

the swooping railway tracks and why
we stole a child like humbugs from the shops.
You twitch and feel the small wet thrill.
You balked, you bottled, ran, that's all.
We heard you from the Policeman's van.
We heard your hands, the short, sharp slaps
of grown-ups clamouring to get back.

# Foreign

Consider abroad, how closely it brushes,
stiffens your skin like the scaly paw
of a fake fur throw when you wake at four
in a cheap hotel; creeps in sly as the hand
up your thigh on the spiralling, narrowing
minaret steps, clammy and moist
as the stump of a limb that's round as a bat
but soft as the skin on the pad of cat's claws.

Think of the smells, the insecticide soaked
through your rucksack, passport; the rubbery
mould on the inside of tents; the medieval streets
with their stink like a phone box; rain
on the dust, that stench of damp dog; the rush
of iron fresh from the butcher's; the stale
of the coppery water in temples, the yellow-
ringed puddles behind great beaten doors.

And noises, the multiple clicks in your mind
like a camera; the howling of prayers
tannoyed from towers; the orders,
the bargains, the beggar's *baksheesh*; flip
flop flip of doors on buses; shrieks
from quarrels you can't understand,
buzzes and flies, the sound of the crowd
rising like water left running for hours.

Above all remember how little this touches,
how by evening it's telly, just small people
miming their hunger and rage. Remember,
against the prospect of mountains, the slice
of a city glimpsed through a window,
to measure that peering in mirrors for sun tans,
the glances in darkened windows of coaches,
searching your face for the difference.

## The Wedding-Guest's Story

Shortly after ditching me, within a matter of weeks,
as I might point out, she bought a remarkable
backless dress and got hitched to an ex-army chap
who climbs up rocks on Sundays: Not the sort,

that chap, if I might explain, to stop for stragglers
or to soak up sun. He'd strike straight for the top
in skin tight kit, lycra shorts and pick, straining
straps around the crotch. In spite of which,

I took my half-meant invite straight, sat tight
throughout, let that dress flash a foot of flesh
to the hushed cathedral, and in my mind
I slowly climbed the low, secret steps of her spine,

swung a spell on my rope in the tuck
of her waist, scrambled sweating, swearing,
over the slopes of her shoulder blades, to
slump on the summit, weak, sobbing with loss.

## Double Take

I imagined that you'd miss me, thought
you'd pace your hardwood floor in odd
worn socks, watch the clock sit stuck,

get late to work, type my name *caps lock*,
press and hold *shift / break*, miss buses, meals,
or sit with fork half way, lost, for minutes,

hours, sleep badly, late, dream chases, shake,
send fingers out to pad the pillow, find
my hollow, start awake, roll over, hug a gap,

an ache, take a walk, damp dawn, of course,
wrapped in your mac, with the collar up, glimpse a slice
of face, tap a stranger's back, draw a blank;

as I have. Each time, I run to press your face
to mine, mine, shining with imagined rain.

# OLIVER COMINS

# Quarry

A family holiday in the nook of childhood:
the dale-head camp site edging on trees
and days marked by periodic rumbling
from the granite quarry downstream.

Town boys with buck voices that set
the air ringing where we fought
for careless power in the bracken
with our chosen staves of ash.

Later, trekking deep into the forest
to chart what territory we'd gained,
we found ourselves adrift in a clearing:
a stag surprised us, breaking from the woods.

Big flank and antler, deer breath.
We resolved to track another glimpse,
presumed enormous woodcraft as we cut
sprigs from trees to wear as horns.

A full week we followed the trail
of our adventure, yarning each other
down stag-ways that didn't exist
while the quarried hillside growled.

Eventually, just a day from home
and scouting the ridge above the stream
for one last time, we reached a hollow
where rock was being cut.

Mid-evening and the place was deserted.
We lobbed stones at an iron hut,
but the sound was lost in the clatter
of stag – bursting from within.

# Floral Clock

An abandoned garden, half-structured wilderness,
where we played domestic games: made our den
in an Anderson shelter, stored food and kindling,
built surreptitious fires that filled the place
with smoke and plotted raids to liberate friends
held prisoner at home by overweening parents.

At one end, the house we never entered, windows
freed of glass and paint work cracking over wood
grown soft to the touch: detritus inside – paper
fallen from the walls, plaster where ceilings
sagged and split in silent rooms, bleak kitchen
with an altar stove, green taps above the sink.

A small orchard at the far end, autumn apples
rotting on the branch or mulching in the grass,
fat blackberries bursting on a bush collapsed
beneath its own weight and dissolute rhubarb
with massive leaves we used as weapons to fight
the flying things that harried through the day.

One long brick wall on which an old rose grew:
dead stems and living intertwined with blooms
from many seasons, hips dried to brown or red
and fresh with seed, new buds almost flowering,
those bright clusters of pink we aimed at with
our lonely catapults, splattering the petals.

## Light Relief

The town smelled of wet stone as rain
swept down from the hills: two shadows
moved slowly on a first floor curtain,
blooming into dance for that moment
when we glanced up from the street.

We crossed the moor with a late night
spinning of yarns: haunted quarries
filled with hollow wind, abbey ruins
where only weather prays and sings,
monstrous sheep staring from the marsh.

Morning found us waiting on a cliff
above an anxious tide as day absorbed
the dark – sun seeped then blossomed
on the sea and someone else's mother
summoned cows, using names of flowers.

# Beside the Seaside

Land here has turned its back on the sea,
but under the towering cliffs a few yards
of shingle negotiate with a garrulous tide.

The woman in the black swimsuit is the most
determined: her powerful voice booms up from
the water's edge against the rock's silence.

Nearby, the children are ignoring mother.
They are learning to screech like gulls,
their thin arms waving bolases of seaweed.

The man would swim but he isn't sure about
that pantomime inside the billowing towel,
or the stomach which mocks his noble legs.

He is poised among robes and carrier bags
waiting to be useful, while a cruel wind
toys with some final strands of hair.

The woman looks at him and turns to dive
full-bodied into the sea, her pink-capped
head surfaces way out beyond the breakers.

A coaster is moving south along the horizon
just like a model, he thinks, suddenly
caught up in the immoderate fun of it all.

# Playing Out Time in an Awkward Light I

*(after a painting by Frank Batson 1901)*

The cool laughter of women drifts over
from the boundary; the Home Farm rookery
has taken to wing above the sight screen,
muffled cacophony intensifying the idyll.
In a moment the ball will leave the hand
of the bowler and seem to float as leather
is gripped by the humid air, then plunge
to a shadowed length where the earth waits
with its own spin. The batsman will hear
the fizz of the ball's flight and its thud
on the wicket as he pushes his bat forward;
he watches, hoping to survive to the end
of the day, but knows it could all be over
in a moment: a voice he does not recognize
calls encouragement from under the trees.

## Playing Out Time in an Awkward Light II

They decided the artist should bat low,
his strokes, they said, were of the wrong kind:
let him sketch events from the boundary
and talk with women in the garden
while we get on with the game.

They were afraid he would not catch the ball
in the field, but he did, and they let him bowl
to keep the game going (they said), but he
kept it tight, so they agreed between them
it was most unlikely he would be needed to bat.

The artist sat below an elm while they played,
he followed the ebb and flow of their manly efforts
and noted the sweet arc of a bat,
the neat crack of a hit in the badinage
of the spectators, who mostly ignored him.

The painter in him enjoyed the leaves' sparkling
in fresh sunlight after rain, resolved a problem
of shadows on a building. The cricketer
knew his moment would come when the game
no longer needed him to make a victory.

He decided he should walk to the wicket
with his easel and a bat: there would be
enough time for him to use both – he would need time
to catch this light, an awkward job,
the others must make allowances for that.

# Playing Out Time in an Awkward Light III

From the library window in the south wing
there is a clear view of the old paddock
where the men have been coming these last
twelve summers for a week of playing cricket,
but I sat there for most of the morning
while wind and drizzle smeared the view.

Indoors, men champed at the bit calling
for sunshine and beer and an early lunch
in case the weather turned – one of them
came to sit with me, but he fell asleep
and I left him there to doze while the sun
began to find its way through the clouds.

When the carpenter arrived with sawdust
they treated him to quantities of wine
I doubt the man has known, but the house
grew quiet before long as they wandered out
in twos and threes to the canvas pavilion,
their striped blazers gleaming with colour.

After lunch I went to the library and read
for most of the afternoon: figures in white
glimmered in the green space above my book,
the game like a dance in the watery light
and their bleak voices raised in unison
seeped into the house from time to time.

Then Mama came round gathering the ladies
to cross the lawn in time for the last hour:
drinks were served as the light began to go
and we chatted with the batsmen whose innings
had been played, their little flashes of wit
more consolatory as the game drew to a close.

# Rural

Reading a book on the bus looks like prayer
from the distance – one head is bowed above
some others that bob and sway, moving with
the road, but only when seats between us
have emptied can I see the object of this
particular attention: a paperback novel
with a sullen cover held open on her lap,
a young face in profile soft with reading.

She seems to be on the point of discovery –
one finger tucking an angle of bobbed hair
sweeps her cheek clear and briefly reveals
a droplet of white pearl on a silver loop.
Not knowing the story but presuming from
the pages that it is too early in the book
for a dénouement, I find myself wondering
what is happening, where it's taking place.

There is the boy: he got on at the same stop
but waits by the exit for their curt farewell,
then crosses the road for a lane by a church
and walks away down a verge of summer grass.
Any fictions of their relationship should be
abandoned for the simple fluke of attending
the same school for a few years and catching
the same bus home through the river villages.

Fields pass, we travel alone with the driver
who stops at a cottage for a box of seedlings.
Her hair has worked its way back from behind
one ear and the finger to her lips is hushing
the final paragraphs of a chapter that will end
with the bus sliding to a halt opposite a line
of shops, a village hall, another darkened pub
with its string of fairy lights in the window.

# Bar Staff

The midnight queue at the bar is ten
years deep, waving notes in a dream
of significance – but we only serve
in strict rotation no one understands.
This one will have lost it all before
the dancing ends – leaving the drink
we've poured in a doorway with lumps
of a meal, he will come to long after
the spillage has been cleared wondering
how the night ended, who did it to him.

His stalling eyes are trying to catch
what's going on beyond the ornate bar,
but they will not see us stop to drink –
we only pause for the measure of air
to struggle through an optic, to show
the bouncers, with a nod of the head,
which of the punters is about to leave
his body behind. Out there in the street
the light is crepuscular orange: a man
sways gently into it, stunned but intact.

# The Coral Club

A covert door in a back-alley,
an Axminster's drowned pattern,
neutral walls primed to glister
and shimmer: the place to come,
just a hint of stale cigarette.

On the empty dance floor black-
suited doormen gather to smoke,
their conversation is riddled
with obscenity, innuendo rising
from springs of harsh laughter.

At ten the switches are thrown,
the club fills with blended light
and a soft opalescence of people
emerging from the reef to feed,
arms trawling the air like cilia.

The admiring eyes of the bouncers
are not obscured by the lasered
dry ice air: some dancers shine
with flower like hauteur, their
clothes the source of limelight.

# Journey

A brisk farewell would not suffice:
you called me back to hold a moment,
gave one distant kiss I think of now,
five thousand hurtled miles later,
queuing for my passport to be stamped.

Waiting in a bar for the hired limo
I take a pale beer, watch foam climb
to the rim of a glass and raise it
in a toast to travelling – an extended
pause before the fluke of arrival.

People move slowly round buildings
in this place, carrying a mind-set
I might grow to share eventually –
being cool in the heat takes time
to learn with unfragmented style.

At home, that hill topped by palms
is covered in grass, not dry scrub
like this, where tumbleweed collects
in a gully and sun beats down
reminding me of my lost shades.

The car lot is bleak as a marsh –
streetlights across water and stark
wires silhouetted on a foreign sky:
I stumble on the thought of you
waiting for our midnight conversation.

# CHRISTINA DUNHILL

# Old People

Wet mouths in dark rooms, old people wait
for a kiss, for a mole on a cheek
to brush your cheek, for you to fall
over their feet splayed out in ancient slippers,
their thick, brown-stockinged, knobbled legs.
Low in overblown floral chairs, they sit
with their enormous khaki handkerchiefs,
dabbing at something.

Old people: they live alone, their green bakelite clocks
tick loud through anything you say, you can't ignore
the patterns on their walls, that tyranny of roses
marching your eye on a meaningless pilgrimage,
again and again and again. They drink brown drinks
from glasses filmy as their eyes; they want you to hold them,
their hands are ready, loose skin, brown spots,
the slippery veins.

Old people, there's always a ball of wool coming from them,
they knit and knit and knit, do darning with mushrooms,
embroider cushions, put smocking on dresses;
they cry in chairs. They leave themselves about in pieces –
three pairs of glasses, three hard snappy cases,
mugs of livid gums with teeth – you look for things
you half expect to find and know you shouldn't;
you don't know what stays in.

Old people want you to hold them together.
They lie in bed and smile and watch
your shaking fingers plait their hair.

# White Wolf

I found your short white hairs
in my bed and laid them side by side.

Four bright hairs on one black sheet
I wanted a fifth for a cross stroke.

I wanted the blood from between your legs
to make communion. I fished it out, dragged

stripes down your flanks to make a rite
to keep you coming back to my bed.

But when you came you were loose and howling,
you cried all night and called me names.

In your sharp brown teeth was a year's debris
so close, you said, bone close.

The next time you came they found us out
and your armpits like swallows couldn't comfort me,

not your smile like a snake's, the slope of your eyes,
your long mouth gone cold to the tongue.

A tree grew up through the floor of my room
and we hung upside down from its branches.

And the next time you came you didn't come at all,
you gave yourself back to the bridebox

your aromatic fur turned nylon, you
crawled back in with a twig in your teeth

lay still, and flapped your lids shut.

# Ring of Kerry

This is the big one, ladies,
the battle of the bedclothes.
Look: in the right hand corner
all our fathers weigh in their bulk,
draw up armchairs and bring out
the Bibles. What's this?
Yours slips in between us
and unzips his trousers
as mine walks away.

As soon as you ask me about
my father, I have nothing
inside at all, but this is
better than that in my mouth.
'Don't put words in my mouth,'
you say. In your head are all
the words anyone ever wanted.
I cannot say anything you do not
know. This is a homecoming.
We are so afraid.

Your pale eyes watch me quiet
like turf, smart as a parable.
Who will take care of us?
they ask. I, said the sparrow,
I am your lover and bold
as a schoolgirl. I know
the answers. I, said the fly,
with my little eye,
I will take care of you.

# Owltime

*for Alison*

The other birds stop when the owls start up
*hú, hu hu hu hu, hu hú*; it is the tawny
and the screech below, *eeeek* like a furred
creature; ah, we used to shout them down,
owls in the zoo, my sister and I, cupping
palms to mouths and hollering *wake up, wykey
wykey! wykey wykey wykey*! If you were lucky
they'd tremble an ear, or scroll down one
ancient lid; they were not pleased, them owls.

It's hunting time, there's bad blood here;
fish-cold at night when the sweating comes,
I'm trying to warm with carnival: oh warm me
with big smiles and skirts, but I only get
gargoyles grinning from boats and then
a blue father doing that – and all I can
blink up to take it away is the limp-haired
Jesus la-la-la-ing by in a barge, trailing
his hands like the Shalott woman.

The trees come right up to the big window
three times eighteen tree-filled panes.
Pay great regard to the birds of the night,
in their time they can take villages,
cantors and rabbis, oxen and carts, chickens
and young wives, lambs at the breast,
swineherds, goatherds, babes in their cots,
swoop them up ribboned like a long-tailed kite.
They could have Hampstead easy as pie.

This is the owltime, eighteen grown tawnies
at eighteen panes hang watching and shimmy
their long-fingered wings; what if I turned
on my pillow to conjure your small curls

and found a sheer white face, a mouthful
of feathers, what if a beak in my mouth said *hú*?
(What if it carried me clean out the window,
wriggling hard as a snake and still writing,
ribboned me on to the village in the sky?)

# Dog Knowledge

There has to be a dog comes home in someone's pocket.
Dad opens his jacket, says look, and you don't know
if it's at the little round-eyed, squeaking thing, or him,
with something there for once where Jesus keeps his red one.

When you get older there's a dog for you to cry with.
My grandmother tells me Sally's a comfort; watch: *boo hoo*.
Up jumps Sally, squirms against her chest and whimpers,
tries to lick her face. Down Gran's village street one day,

the builder's dog detained me, leapt up in a fit of humour,
knocked me down and sat on me. He didn't get up.
No one passed by. His wagging tail kept thumping me.
I had to wait till he grew bored. His *what*? my mother said.

My barmy gran won't let you say *shut*; tooth the flesh off
    oranges;
'develop'. She hid behind the kitchen door, impaled the peaks
of my new Winfield Junior (28) on two outstretched index fingers.
Good! she said, (the cones collapsed). *No bosoms in this family*.

I knew girls who longed to be dogs – get some attention,
bit of respect. And mums who said, when told there wouldn't be
a man (No, Mum, not now, not any day): *It'll be animals next*.
Catch me at Clissold Park, following chows – they have

the friskiest, curliest, jauntiest bums you ever saw.

# To One of Her Sisters

The curtains have parted, pink silk damask, wine velvet;
Look at us, hair scraped so high it hurts from forehead
To ear. We're white with a powder whose sweetness clogs
The air. Oh, we are proper as a quire of paper
And ten quills, strait as a sonata in the drawing room.
Look at us, naked as piglets. Tell me, sister,
When those slow fingers last unbuttoned breeches,
Those rosy nails scored an ostler's flanks?
Quick dearest! a nipple – that tiny mount tender
As the frosted tip of a sweetmeat. Tell me of venery!

(*'Gabrielle d'Estrées et une de ses soeurs'*,
*School of Fontainebleau, 18th cent.*)

# The Darts

The darts were faithful like hawks.
The picture of them on the box was faithful
to what lay inside. Three new darts with orange flights
in velveted plastic grooves. The metal gleamed.

Their perfect grips, each tiny steel bubble firm,
each indentation clean, asked for your fingers.
You'd crowd and splay the single fronds along
your cheek, then smooth them back.

The moment when you took them lightly
and raised them to your ear, contained the moment
when your eye and wrist would drive them home –
a pledge. No extraneous movement.

The hair on my arms hadn't grown yet
but there was no doubt I'd be a man one day.

# Andrew Hardie's Girls and Boys

Watch any group of people, says Mr Hardie,
you'll see they walk, right *and*, right *and* –
then wonder why they've got one leg longer than the other.
Andrew Hardie dancers *stand on two legs*.
Don't *loaf!* says Mr Hardie. Don't let me catch you loafing
with one hip out. Remember, you're a dancer all the time.
     – And don't walk on your feet.

See us pink and leafy girls go fervent on the stair,
our hush and whispers, tiny giggles, nudges from cold arms.
Watch us check and pin our cleavages, descend, then enter,
tall and turned out, patting hairstyles, scratch and scrape
our fish soles in the resin, swing one *whole life's labour*
'beautiful' long ballet leg behind us to our heads,
     and pull the foot to our hairgrips.

     We're Andrew Hardie's girls and boys –
     'Ladies, gentlemen and others . . .
     take then your second position.
     Thank you, Miss Barnard.'
     'Thank *you*, Mr Hardie,' says Miss Barnard –
     when she's feeling saucy –
     aiming a sigh at Sebastian
     as her fingers hit the keys.

Andrew Hardie's girls and boys exhibit perfect placement.
We don't distort. Our hips are never lifted.
Our spines are pulled down to the lowest vertebra.
We turn out from the hip, not the foot.
Our shoulders drop softly away from our necks.
Our arms are raised high on wide backs.
     Our working feet are tight as claws.

     Mr Hardie likes the girls
     but in a joyful moment, trying
     to get a blush; he'll sing:

    *Oh, the boy across the river*
    *has a bottom like a peach,*
    *but alas I cannot swim.*

All the world together, says Mr Hardie, in the centre –
he likes to speak in mock translations from the French.
He shuffles to the battered gilt-framed mirror
his square face, square jacket, old square trousers,
arranges in a child's fifth his enormous Oxfords, coughs,
fingers the frayed edge of his jacket sleeves,
    demonstrates perfect *épaulement*.

## Denise Delieu

I'm watching you
watch your two trained feet come snug together,
pursing the close of your pirouette, only slightly clacking.
Your tongue slides back behind your teeth,
a hint of pink blancmange,
your mouth suggests a smile.
No one should watch their feet but when a glance
can bring such happiness, who'll blame you?
Counter staff spend all day long
watching the rings on their fingers.

When you come skipping down the stairs
we watch to see how you've done your hair;
it's said you keep a hairdresser's folder of styles.
Your French pleat sometimes wins applause.
Good morning, Denise, says Mr Hardie
and all the girls are jealous
of your pink mouse feet scuffling in the resin.
You're the one they'd get to model the Virgin;
we're just the water for your nymph to look in.

Once you'd have gone tripping into class
at the Miss Abigail Bussingham School of Dance,
vanity case, hair bouncing in elastic and ribbons;
practising turn-out. Out of class, you'd wear white T-straps
to parties and to Sunday school. You'd get all the stamps
and lick them in just so, tight in their frames,
no sloppy over-moisturising.
You'd carry a white Bible, gilt letters and trim,
keep those grey eyes quietly on your feet
and no one would know it wasn't modesty.

Denise Delieu, I used to run away from girls like you –
some pyjama case girl might zip me in,
a rabbit girl, a pussycat girl – ears, tail and whiskers –
the girl shape in the wardrobe.

# Ballet Girl

One day you hear it: *Hello* in a cherry drop smile.
Why not become one of us baseless girls,
with the point of a top to spin from instead of feet?
Take the fingers of your beau, twirl an eternal pirouette
in some drifting never-never, swirling snowflakes,
    paperweight.

Become one of us wronged and moral fairy girls,
looking for food, a little cottage, the gardener, the path,
the other half of the ring from the fish's mouth.
Caught in dripping satin, muslin, lengths of fur,
our gloved hands, seeking pies, find skylark nests,
our slippered feet mole blind until the swans jump into
    forests.

Join the toys who come to life at midnight
wound up to twirl and shimmy, clamour, sing
a shanty for our supper, drill and bang
our drums until we shudder, cry real tears, fall flat,
hard on our keys. That's showbiz!
Give us that tune again. Didn't you love us!

Remember every single photo in that polyfoto session.
Do exactly what I say: right arm out, now left, right hand
up as if for teacher; look down, look at the ceiling.
*Smile*. Don't look so worried. *Now!* Be a ballet girl.
Get thin, get lost, get lovely. Become adorable.

# Say 'Moose' for Me

I want to pull you back to say 'moose' for me
with that double 'o' sound, each 'o' single, separate,
hanging perfect in the air like smoke rings
two 'o's suspended, soft in the back palate like an owl –
like that poem by Elizabeth Bishop: *A moose
has come out of the impenetrable wood.*

Things you didn't say to me
in your wry New England undertone,
move into my mind, hunching their shoulders.
I run back through time. I'll carry your books.
Let's both go paddling your canoe, I'll be in your camp,
we'll practise pissing though a tap. Talk to me.

You were pretty as the woodcutter's daughter
fresh as the third son out for his fortune
good day, good morrow, madam, sir, a feast,
a meeting in the forest.
You left me alone in a wood at night
where the trees gang up and mutter.

Your perfect absence, nothing else would do.
You drove off, a mad coachman beating the horse,
turning and grinning from between your sideburns.
And something else ran in front of my car, tiny feet
faster than clockwork: a mouse in the headlights,
desperate for shadows.

## The Shape of Her

Somewhere a woman prepares to love another woman
for the first time and wonders: is she ready?

Going to love a woman is not like going to buy a dog.
She will not squeal and waggle her behind,

she will not pounce and jump on you. She will not pause
under the dwindling cherry blossom and catch the petals

to stick them on her nails, she will not sing *tirra lirra*
*I don't know. Wait for the chill birdsong of evening.*

She won't dwell in a Hotel Room, half-dressed,
reading Trollope in the daytime, like Edward Hopper, 1913.

She is not Cindy Sherman, lying on the floor with her dress
rolled up to her face: she is alive. There is no saying

what she'll say. Perhaps she does not want you. Here is
the shape of her. She is not a wardrobe, she is not

a box of toffee, she is not a pillow of cloud,
an old Baird wireless, nor a handsome Chesterfield. She is not

the Encyclopedia Britannica; you will ask her things she
    cannot
answer; she will ask you what you're doing, you won't know.

You want to be her monkey, her mother, her lover, her beau,
her favourite aunt, little sister, toyboy, her big brother,

her box of Liquorice Allsorts, her dressing-up cupboard,
her joke polyurethane apron, Lady Penelope's pink

Rolls Royce, her gold cupid, her Sugar Puff engine,
her Swamp Thing, her fat grunting hog on a rope.

# ALICE OSWALD

# A Greyhound in the Evening
# After a Long Day of Rain

Two black critical matching crows,
calling a ricochet, eating its answer,

dipped
      home

and a minute later
the ground was a wave and the sky wouldn't float.

       \*

With a task and a rake,
with a clay-slow boot and a yellow mac,
I bolted for shelter under the black strake dripping of timber,

summer of rain, summer of green rain
coming everywhere all day down
through a hole in my foot.

       \*

Listen listen listen listen

       \*

They are returning to the rain's den,
the grey ones, rolling up their veils,
taking the steel taps out of their tips and heels.

Grass lifts, hedge breathes,
rose shakes its hair,
birds bring out all their washed songs,
puddles like long knives flash on the roads.

       \*

And evening is come with a late sun unloading a silence,
tiny begin-agains dancing on the night's edge.

But what I want to know is
whose is the great grey wicker-limbed hound,
like a stepping on coal, going softly away . . .

## Pruning in Frost

Last night, without a sound,
a ghost of a world lay down on a world,

trees like dream-wrecks
coralled with increments of frost.

Found crevices
and wound and wound
the clock-spring cobwebs.

All life's ribbon frozen mid-fling.

Oh I am
stone thumbs,
feet of glass.

Work knocks in me the winter's nail.

I can imagine
Pain, turned heron,
could fly off slowly in a creak of wings.

And I'd be staring, like one of those
cold-holy and granite kings,
getting carved into this effigy of orchard.

# Gardeners

Damp of sleeve, working inattentively,
naming insects, gauging the sky,

considering the life
and knocking the mud off,

in a through-place of rooks and wagtails
and cloud-shadows like slow pterodactyls,

they bent low, they lamented the weather;
the sun picked and chose like a fault-finder

and it rained on the kale pots
and the wind belaboured the cabbage nets.

They with round backs
carried the hours like peat sacks,

dug perfect cubes,
despised office jobs

and tossed the rotten one
and took the barrows in

and saw two men talking intently
and whistled softly and went on steadily.

# The Glass House

The glass house is a hole in the rain,
the sun's chapel,
a bell for the wind.


Cucumbers, full of themselves,
the long green lungs of that still air,


image the fruits of staying put,
like water-beetles in woodland puddles
and hoofprints.


And I
am a hole in the glass house,
taking my time between the rows.


The leaves, the yellow blooms, the pots
vanish through a loop of thoughts.


Then far off
comes the cluck-sound of this green can
dipping and spilling . . .
and dipping again.

# Sleep

Now our close heads, like under a gravestone,
are intact and locked. We turn,
in the thrift of sleep, each to his own;

negotiate in the same place,
one feat – the sucking and blowing
eight hours of air at a steady pace.

Imagine – you who can leap a gate
feet together with one hand on the bar
and swing to a halt for a second as you float, . . .

in many kinds, in cobwebs, under wings,
on paws, in shells, the breathing enters you
into a unity of drowsing things;

and when I wake, the only sound's a sequel
of absurd tasks – this heaviness of air
and how you roll it uphill and downhill.

# When a Stone Was Wrecking His Country

When a man went to fight a stone,
he clenched his knuckle-stones, he lifted his foot-stones,
he upheld himself like the last megalith,
he kissed his lady like a white abandonable sea-pebble,
he felt as justified as a set slate.

He saw the sky like an open flint
and the starlings fallen and shaken about like gravel.
He wanted to go carefully like making a wall.
He went as far as meteorites disappear
into the holes and shadows of the universe like a curious
    pumice.

Went among tree boughs like the dark detail of marble,
went among animals like various amethysts
and men of rock and flowers extempore as lava
and came to confusion like a heap of shale.
He came to despair like moisture coming up through chalk.

He had to oppose everything, he had to grind away
at his own tooth-stones, saying:
'if I could sift the silicate from these bones,
if this complexion of feldspar,
if this ego-dragon spiralling like a fossil . . . '

but he couldn't rest like a little grit under an eyelid
till his head like some god-in-a-boulder
rolled from its purpose and came down among stone-kind.

# The Melon Grower

She concerned him,
but the connexion had come loose.
They made shift with tiffs and silence.

He sowed a melon seed.
He whistled in the greenhouse.
She threw a slipper at him

and something jostled in the loam
as if himself had been laid blind.
She misperceived him. It rained.

The melon got eight leaves, it lolled.
She banged the plates.
He considered his fretful webby hands.

'If I can sex,' he said, 'the flowers,
very gently I'll touch their parts
with a pollen-brush made of rabbit hairs.'

The carpels swelled. He had to prop them on pots.
She wanted the house repainting.
He was out the back watering.

He went to church, he sang 'O Lord how long shall the wicked . . . ?'
He prayed, with his thumbs on his eyes.
His head, like a melon, pressured his fingers.

The shoots lengthened
and summer mornings came with giant shadows
and arcs as in the interim of a resurrection.

She stayed in bed, she was coughing.
He led the side-shoots along the wires.
She threw the entire tea-trolley downstairs.

And when the milk was off
and when his car had two flat tyres
and when his daughter left, saying she'd had enough,

he was up a ladder, hanging soft nets from the beam
to stop the fruit so labouring the stem.
The four globes grew big at ease

and a melony smell filled the whole place
and he caught her once, confused in the greenhouse,
looking for binder-twine. Or so she says.

# The Thing in the Gap-Stone Stile

I took the giant's walk on top of world,
peak-striding, each step a viaduct.


I dropped hankies, cut from a cloth of hills,
and beat gold under fields
for the sun to pick out a patch.


I never absolutely told
the curl-horned cows to line up their gaze.
But it happened, so I let it be.


And annual meadow grass, quite of her own accord,
between the dry-stone spread out emerald.


(I was delighted by her initiative
and praised the dry-stone for being contrary.)


What I did do (I am a gap)
was lean these elbows on a wall
and sat on my hunkers pervading the boulders.


My pose became the pass across two kingdoms,
before behind antiphonal, my cavity the chord.


And I certainly intended
anyone to be almost
abstracted on a gap-stone between fields.

# April

The sheer grip and the push of it – growth gets
a footledge in the loosest stems, it takes
the litterings of weeds and clocks them round;
your eyeballs bud and alter and you can't
step twice in the same foot – I know a road,
the curve throws it one way and another;
somebody slipped the gears and bucketed slowly
into the hawthorns and his car took root
and in its bonnet now, amazing flowers
appear and fade and quiddify the month;
and us on bicycles – it was so fast
wheeling and turning we were lifted falling,
our blue-sky jackets filling up like vowels . . .
and now we float in the fair blow of springtime,
kingfishers, each astonishing the other
to be a feathered nerve, to take the crack
between the river's excess and the sun's.

# A Wood Coming into Leaf

From the first to the second,

*

warily, from the tip to the palm,

*

third leaf (the blackthorn done)

*

from the fourth to the fifth and
(Larix, Castanea, Fraxinus, Tilia)

*

Thaw taps, groping in stumps,
Frost like an adder easing away . . .

*

the sixth to the seventh (plums conceive
a knobble in a stone within a blossom)

*

ushers the next by the thumbs to the next . . .

*

a thirty-first, a thirty-second,

*

a greenwood through a blackwood
passes (like the moon's halves
meet and go behind themselves)

      *

and you and I, quarter-alight, our boots in shadow,

      *

Birch, Oak, Rowan, Ash
chinese-whispering the change.

# My Neighbour, Mrs Kersey

That noise, Mrs Kersey – were you listening?
A tin roof warping and booming . . .

Our sitting-rooms connect like shears
into the screw-pin of our fires.

We share a bird's nest in a common chimney.
If I'm right, you breathe, Mrs Kersey,

close as a dream-self on the other side.
This wall, if you just rubbed an eyelid,

is a bricked up looking-glass.
And wind across that roof's a loss

of difference to whatever's moving
privately through our heads this evening.

Like the clicking of my door,
the tic-tac of your solitaire.

# Sonnet

When I sit up this late, breathing like so
into the growing soap-ball of my silence,
I just can't think and I don't want to know
whether I've lost my heart to my resilience;
not care, not speak – the clock, the book, the chair
and this one self, beyond sufficiency,
gone like an oyster to the ocean's floor
to make of love the pearl's cold quality . . .
I chose to think of you but I can't say
whether it's peace or makeshift that I live
in this last zero of the millionth day
which ends like this, just breathing to survive.
And I don't know and so I haven't said
whether it's you or nothing in my head.

# Woman in a Mustard Field

From love to light my element
was altered when I fled
out of your house to meet the space
that blows about my head.

The sun was rude and sensible,
the rivers ran for hours
and whoops I found a mustard field
exploding into flowers.

And I slowly came to sense again
the thousand forms that move
all summer through a living world
that grows without your love.

# RICHARD PRICE

# The Fionas

'Fiona', that's a name so Scottish, so
compelling. The Fionas I love,
and used to love (a swingpark
in that comfortable housing estate,
colours of their anoraks), the low
voices of Fionas in their teens,
intimate as the flirts
my elder brothers were, the fights,
the neatness of the jeans of Fionas,
the lazy ache of too much –
the taste of her mouth is the taste
in the mouth – French kissing,
the scent of a girl
on your lambswool sweater
those miles after parting.
Fiona, Fiona, Fiona.

NOTE   *The name 'Fiona' did not exist before the 1890s,*
*when it was invented by Paisley man William Sharp. Sharp,*
*sometime friend of Yeats and member of the Rhymers' Club,*
*wrote several volumes of short stories and poems based in the*
*Highlands and Islands and peppered with spurious*
*Gaelicisms. His pseudonym was 'Fiona Macleod'.*

## Saying the swim

I am in the two of us at the breast stroke,
our hair flat, black, painted,
your eyes darker and larger, shining,
and the pool is not now municipool –
the sink and the Atlantic –
and swallowing and breathing are shuffling
the air between the banknotes in our leather lungs –
you look and choke, tread water, glisten,

cough,

you are in the two of us at the crawl,
our heads down, blundering, shaking
a sheet of water, a duvet between us,
snapping up the air,
a bedcover patterned with swimming,
and the two of us folding ourselves over,
sinking and slightly rolling, coming up, all out,
under, sinking and rolling,

the two of us in the two of us,
swimming

## 'Skirt'

Feet more delicate than yours
slant out from the duvet.
On the carpet a skirt
catches its breath;
that scent you avoid
pretends it's *déjà vu*.

My hands, I trust,
are not someone else's.

## With is

To ravel with you in ripening light.
To worry and adore
the stacking cups of your spine.

What I come with
is a dubious country,
a prejudice against people like us:
nationals who've dropped to couples,
two martens agog
under a tired Scots pine.

Our table is empty,
a summer curling pond.
Come on out on the town!
I've the nightbus map
you lent me
when I was only a Scot.

# Block

When you carved me
this was the hand
you gave me to give you,
breath in the smoothness
of worked rock.

Away from you,
I'm worried –
back into the block:
the erratic that's me
gets rough, rolls
like an ending cam.

The ice has me
under its thumb:
I'm back,
in the earth's stone,
north.

Is that the warmth
of your mouth?

# Sense and a minor fever

Curtains breathing, books not clapping,
drying clothes surround us.
I can hear an overtaking,
the grind of a train of heaps,

and here's you, sleeping,
irritable, sifting the air
as if there was a hair
at the back of your tongue,

as if your lungs were listening to me
with your heart's healthy scepticism.

# Stopper

At the front of the top deck
we're some kind of couple.

Through the smear
a harmonica's bad teeth
smile on a shelter's roof.
A woman leans
to keep her Alsatian.
All solicitors
keep cactuses
in teapots.

No, lean your way,
touch my sleeve
if you see anything I miss.

## A new establishment

A sudden weekend.

A friend fresh out of marriage
electrifies our entry-phone;
a backing-singer
pushed to a solo mike.

In our mucky hall
our parents' children's books
buzz like two-stroke engines.
One of us talks down.

When the storm door waives
man-made soles
flap breathily up the steps . . .

Later, our visitor in the close again,
the bracelet, the doorchain, is fast.
I unsaddle separates
from the bandy clothes-horse.

On the stereo
a single's black coffee
twirls its central cream.
Like a love-letter

we fold the bedcover.

# Glinchy

He'd peel a golfball with a penknife
he'd found on a river-strand
and cured with wire wool.

There'd be bets
the ball'd not strip
in a oner,
and they'd be right –
golfballs are not oranges –
but the single white skin
was in Glinchy's hands
at the upshot.
'A hole in one.'

The inside was elastic
twined tight
like a statistic
for nylon
knitted round the globe.
He'd pluck it to unreel it,
a kind of music,
test it in his arms' span,
then stretch it
road wide between lamp-posts.

On the boulders of a rockery
we'd all sit back
waiting for the ambling car.

The elastic always snapped,
but the driver clocked the tension,
the line on the windscreen
tightening.

Glinchy'd say:
*It wizny uz.*

# A forest

I'm back, and the air's around me,
lungs in the pink again,
a sense of the height of the beeches,
the pines, the birches,
millions of years in their company
but fresh when the breeze is flirting.

The ground holds everything
so my footprints are my memory.
No lookbacks though, just following –
finding my path find its falling.

Holly-trees have clawed
darkness into their leaves,
their burden.
Reddish ragged robins
in the uncleared clearing
make light of their ribbons.
I know the pale undersides
of the leaves of wild raspberries,
the tough but flowering
tumbles of bramble,
how fungus is wood
but also leather,
how nettles don't tremble
except together, a tactic.

I know the long chassis,
its cab all twisted
on its stiffened shoulder,
the ground just glass
in the state of powder,
the ash.

# Tie-breaker

### 1

You are an islander with skin cancer.
Outline the history of the petrochemical industry.

### 2

You are a four-year-old with asthma.
Explain the theory of traffic calming.

### 3

In a phrase of not more than ten words
justify water.

*Employees, their friends and their relatives
are not eligible for this competition.*

*No correspondence will be entered into.
The judge's decision is final.*

## At a Mary

At a nunnery with dishcloths
the tat-racks have our minutes.

Drizzle.

Up the smudged hill, a Mary,
praying or diving. Being white.

Tablet-slabby the path, not a path
a stream. Rhododendrons

dripping not sniffing.

Fluff-warm in our layers of wool,
in our blue cagouls; breathing that.

The rocks are giant steps, juds,
gravel's on the flags.

The seeping,

the wet woody light, the leggy shrubs.
We're you and I, pushing the slope

up the slope – into the open,
the tumbling grass, the slapped rocks.

Gusts.

All the hills are with us
there and there, and higher.

We are Nature Lovers; think highly.
Within her railings, streaky Mary:

drenched.

We're stepping up, taking the plinth.
Two black goats

can't finish their mouthfuls.
Scare / dismissal?

Hefty and gone.

# MIKE VENNER

# When My Ship Comes In

At last it was on the horizon, a big three-islander, and it was coming in.

I waited on the sand with the sandflies pricking my ankles. I smiled. My ship.

Still it came, but as it came somehow it wasn't getting any bigger.

Perhaps it had stopped. No, I can see it clearer now, rigging and wash.

I could almost make out the captain, red in the face from sun and yelling.

I waited, and still it came, clearer, frothing at the bow, getting no bigger.

I had only to wait, so I waited, and my ship came in, shrinking and shrinking.

The tide washed it right up to my feet. I picked it up. Shook the sea out.

Held it to my ear to hear the captain's hello. Listened hard. No hello. No captain.

Carefully I returned it to the sea and shoved it off and watched it leave.

Slow at first, and then full ahead, making a coot's wake, a swan's wake,

ship's wake, ship's wake, and soon it was miles away, growing as it went.

# Cauliflower Truck Incident Riddle

Wiltshire hills got it, shouldered it off the road onto its side,
its load tumbling into the ditch. Silence while Nature adjusts
itself to this event, taking a moment or two to make sense of it,
plugging it well in before switching back on, then curses heard,
alien-sounding, and big men begin to pull one another out.

They wear white oversuits and helmets, the uniform of all
cauliflower-men. Possibly from some small town in Brittany,
a land which reeks of cauliflowers, the stench so strong there
they have to carry their own air. Guns too to keep us peasants off
when such accidents happen, the theft of one single head

being a capital offence in more ways than one. But even so,
us peasants come, clustering civilian wallies, forelocks
all tugged-out, looking for food, excitement, or perhaps
ornaments for our agricultural cottages. The spacemen
slap the matt flanks of their weapons. Peasants scattering

like rooks, uttering feral cries. Spacemen alone again.
Alone with their cauliflowers they gaze at the hills,
bare but for the odd tuft of coppicing – by these tufts
the hills may be grasped. One or two men are tempted to run
for the brush and cower in it. Fear stops them.

Fear of being ripped apart by birds. Of deer. Of starting
an animal riot, panic in the landscape. Fear of setting
something off. A life spent carrying cauliflowers
can give a man strange dreams. He fears so many things.
Naked hillsides, sudden noises, an unblinking eye.

He clings to his charges, holding them close as hostages,
as close as a parent holding a favourite child, proud,
yet somehow fearful that it may go off Pop! and silence him
for good. Bang goes his hope for the future. Bang goes
posterity, bang goes everything, bang, bang, bang, bang.

# Dressing Up

Today I'm in black. A black peg. A lean
gunslinger flashing heat at soft ladies.
Do I make you dream cemeteries?
Do I brand you with the imprint of my bones,
my hot wires? If so I must be kissed
and then run out of town.

Today I'm in pink, a flabby toddler big as a room.
I rock villages, crush grown-ups where I pass.
Beware my gaa-gaa goo-goo: this deep sloppiness
has too many ways of getting out. My gums
have been known to remove limbs. My yearning drool
at first anaesthetizes, then dissolves flesh.

Today I'm in white, a bathroom suite,
and I will wash you till you don't know who you are.
Yes, white, white, loony white, dream white, pure
white like pain, white like blood in black-and-white
is black, like black pain, black intestinal
dark, a white so white you're as good as blind.

Today I wear a suit of lights. A skin-tight
mirror membrane makes the world curl
about my limbs in rivulets of every colour.
I rattle hot ampoules at passing bulls. By night
I gleam in the wings, and flashing diode switches
mark out the routes by which I wish to be touched.

But tomorrow I'm going to go green. I want to crack
ice-crusts, snort frost, eat sun, grow fat on its fire
and look fantastic against the sky. I want to die
with the wind shaking the breath out of me,
live again, die again, live again, but always live
within my leaf, within the ambience of death.

## A Sense of Place

When a moon pulls, seas are supposed to come so far
and then pull back, or else they flop off into space.
But mine, much lived-in, drowned-in, for too long
held in balk, thirsty for a sudden lunge
at nothingness or, to put it another way,
hungry for anything, as I say, my seas simply

swarm out, slosh off through the stratosphere,
icebergs and all, leaving a parched and pitted planet,
the wide I-told-you-so eye of the stranded whale.
Some fish went into orbit. Most burst.
Some of the ships went all the way
and wrecked themselves on lunar rocks.

I was born in Berks, Maidenhead, between Staines
and Slight Spotting, very nearly Sloughed. My dad died
in a shell-burst when I was nothing. My first dream
was of a long room lined with fancily-panelled doors
which were all wall as soon as I tried to get out.
I dreamed it again and again until, one fair dawn,

I was woken by a tinkling troupe of players who came
and cut my belly open, much as you would gut a fat turbot,
leaving hideously pleasurable gifts on the coverlet.
They had stamped them with butterflies. When I reached,
my touch turned them back into Golly and Elly. Only
the sheep's teeth that I kept close to my face at night

clung on, holding in the breath of magic that had killed
and healed me all in one. There is a third dream:
a dark bundle on a parachute drifts down
in utter silence, never landing: it is my man,
my Hiroshima Big Boy, my own name. No sign of a plane.
No friendly Biggles dropped it. It still falls. And falls

only in England, where I live, even when I'm well away.
England, my dead whale, my sooty mantle with the pretty
postcard words, my oyster, my gutterful of wet confetti.
I feel English, think English, think I think too much,
too much information, too little actual knowledge, detect,
in the seriousness of my condition, not much gravity.

Swayed, at times, yes, by natural forces, rivers, seas.
But if hills, grass, trees earth me, my thick house
keeps them at bay. Outside, the birds, but inside I hear
the TV cry because no one has turned it on. My own God
holds good, but religion is glib, a suspiciously neat fit.
Truth seldom naked, so often nude. Words struggle up

through thought, much as electricity struggles in thin
tungsten veins, the glass globe containing enough
of the heat-fit to make light. And this light is dim,
European, English, yellow. Lurks behind white nets
where dim things move. Tramps want to come in
and lay hands on my wine, my careful artefacts.

Do they know how it is to have flat bone-words
press upon you, clatter out through letter slots,
how liquids flow off them? As gravestones go
they can be very grave. Like stones, it takes rain
to make them shine. My best self needs no rain,
but if rained on loves to get full, and even drown.

Oh, how are we to survive such grand self-images?
Shall we all be jolly to the core? Shall we waggle wings
till they wrench off us? Shall we play at love till our eyes
pop their sockets and fall on grass? (And then dib them in,
dib-dib, and hope they grow – blooms, babies, cabbages,
hostages against extinction, same as words . . . )

Let's play. Play at being Edisons, unsunned, flesh puttied
into black recesses, addicts of the critical flash, proud

of the retinal scars that mark the moments where
we came alive. Let's whip up some words, heat wires, set fire
to fingers to find the limits of this darkened room, and when
the real sun comes, close our eyes and hope to burn.

How else do we find our sense of place,
those of us that seem to have no place,
whose roots are all skin and dream?
Where is home, the centre of peace,
for those of us who must first
burst before we really belong?

# The Bike

You left your bike when you left me,
chained to the tree outside in the street
with a chain so thick no junkie could cut it,
and rustless against the biting rain.

I tried to file it, spent hours with the combination
for the sake of the tree, for Me for godsake,
and for the dogs: no tree should have a metal friend,
no dog can decide which bit to cock a leg on.

You might have left me the number, Imogen.
You had my socks, you took the stereo.
I'm left with your bike, and broken bits of me
(mostly the bits that write abrasive poetry.

Here's a typical couplet:
'Please come back to me, O subject of a thousand sonnets;
collect your bloody velocipede and have a smash-up on it.')

And then the bike began to go,
taking its time, most of winter.
Invisible autumn hands reduced it,
pump first, then lights,
bell, saddlebag, saddle,
front brake, handlebars,
mudguards, chain and pedals.

Or was it you, creeping up in the night with a spanner?
Have you lost the combination too?
Did it dissolve into a mess of slippery digits
in the acid of our parting?
No. I know. Not you. No chance. He's rich, the sod,
he's got two cars, who needs a bike.

Some weeks ago the back wheel went.
Today, at last, the frame has gone.

This is the way a bicycle travels
when left to its own devices.
I imagine every bit of it is now
grafted onto other bikes all over town,
and every nasty little bit of it is busy
CHANGING ALL THE OTHER BIKES.

The front wheel is still chained to the tree –
rather a fine beech in fact –
and dogs piss through the spokes, no problem.

# The Passage of Spring

1   *Spring Comes Downstream*

Some way up the valley a girl fell in and drowned.
She hadn't been raped, nor stabbed in a jealous fit,
nor was she pregnant with the landlord's child.
She had fancied rinsing her feet after stepping in some shit.
She had slipped, and bashed her head, gone under and died.

This was almost at the foot of Eggardon, an old hill fort,
where the water, hardened by the bones of fallen men,
is at its best and chalkiest. There'd also been
a couple of thunderplumps in the night, so the stream
was somewhat swollen too. Pity no one thought to bottle it:
some will kill for a vial of virgin storm-water . . .
And the stream lost no time Pooh-sticking her off
(or swanning her away, if you prefer),
while licking the life out of her.

Nothing to announce her coming, but the tell-tale
susurrus of rustic poets unpocketing their quills.
And then, inside Eggardon, a big bell sounded dimly,
and the landscape shook itself awake. Farmlands
rippling, hills tumescing, the old earth
soiled itself in excitement, and some animals
were thrilled into giving birth.

There was news of a new type of cruise
for smaller beasts. An orchestra of fleas
struck up on deck in the hopes that this ship
was no Titanic, and the mice hopped on and danced.
And the plants: how pleased they seemed, how proud;
how they hurra-ed and Mexican-waved as she passed.
What girl would not have been glad to have caused
such a ruckus, such a luscious how-do-you-do?

Soon green had all its machines on,
crashing gears in a hurry to bud.
The sun got its guns out and the land began to panic.
Roots reached out blindly for the heart
and slit tree-bark spat blood.

Leaves sprayed out with the crackle of automatics,
and bushes burst like grenades.
There was talk of jets. Next
the oaks were land-mining our favourite walks
and we were suddenly cluster-bombed by a billion seeds.

A strange warm gas rose from the soil and clung to flowers,
napalm of green, green. Then a whole hill went nuclear.

She was coming. It was war, and no one knew why.

2   *Clearing a Passage*

I have come to this large house with the long lawn
to fix a price for clearing the stream. It can't be much.
They're not really rich. We'll ignore the fear in his eyes
as he jokes: 'Wouldn't want a dead nymph to get stuck
at the bottom of my garden. She must float on.'

I tried him on five, we fixed on four, plus
'all the strawberries you can eat. So bad for our arthritis.
And us too arthritic to pick them. Better get 'em
before the badgers do.' He offered me a spade, a sickle,
a pruning saw. I demurred. Even had my own wellies.

Better make a start. Climbed down through huge nettles,
stepped in, up to my thighs, cold, but the top
half of me still in sweat. Slipped a bit, shorts wet,
grabbed the fallen willow and called the hills to heel.
The world came down to my level. It was time to grin.

Soft as a tide of cats, this stream simply never stopped,
aloof from its envelope, holding its coldness
against anything the sun could do. I understood.
I was ready for the dragonfly, razor-blue,
making deep nicks in the air's flesh. Ready

for the crass sluggishness of the horsefly
and the nudge of eel. Ready to be jugged-up
by foaming blossoms and drown in thin sky. Ready
to float by like a dead lady with lungfuls of grubs,
bloated and ghostly as a gas sandwich. Grab the spade.

Begin slicing the ooze, levering leaking clods of it
over my shoulder into the field, where it splats
like cow-pats. The thin seep of water in a mush of reed
and weed becomes a mass, beginning to heave things
out of its way amid thunderclouds of mud. The stream

is a machine starting to work itself, a stuck pump
only needing oil and a whack from a canny plumber.
The fieldside bank is soon clear, down as far
as the fallen willow. Threads of mud show how
it goes on attending to its own streamlining.

Some of the greenery needs thinning out. Clumps of reed
to be yanked out of bed and hurled away like bolas.
Giant hellebore tending to fall in where the roots
are too close to the edge. Big nettles which lean down
and seem to squirt at you well before sting touches skin.

I will now deal with the willow. Testing the saw,
somehow cut my hand and the blood won't stop.
Suck, spit, suck, spit, my own blood threading
downstream, and the stream streaming into me
through the cut. Far too late for the TCP.

The stream and me, we are brothers by now, we have
each other's diseases. Suck, spit, suck, spit. This
is the way we kiss down here. I may even become a frog,

a green *grenouille* called Saul, and *saule* is a willow,
I'm dreaming and sawing at the same time; suck, spit,

suck, spit, says the saw with its teeth in the tree.
It cuts easily, but the severed branches refuse
to come out of the water, excalibured-in.
I balance myself on a boulder and pull with both arms.
Slowly, slowly one of them comes up. This branch has hair!

Instead of leaves, each twig is wigged with underwater roots,
sucking water as a sun substitute. Its weight
is suddenly explained to me as a shaggy *tête de nègre*
breaks free of the mud and leaps out at me,
knocking me flat back into the water. I struggled up,

weighed down by weed and this hideous root. Did snakes
nest in this? A big nettle swam slobbishly through my legs
and stung me underwater. I think I yelled. Took a while
to calm down. It was only a willow. It could be cut,
it could be pulled, it could be floated ashore in chunks.

And this is what I did. And the stream swelled.
As the mud cleared it showed boulders. Too heavy to lift.
They had to be rolled through the water. I'll build a wall
where the inlet is, on the garden side, randomly,
walking them up one by one and rocking them in till they fit.

Downstream there is a clump of arum lilies.
I have muddied their trumpets and must wash them.
And so I do. A small segment of twig is lodged
inside one of them, at the base of the long yellow stamen.
I fear to touch it. I will have to shake it out.


3   *And Breaking Lilies*

She pushes into a thick bed of reeds and cress some way above
the passage I have cleared for her

Here the water starts to creep from under her body seeping
through webs of root and weed and the water-meadow presses in
to suck the stream of its storm-force

She passes on sluggishly now through grasses as if borne along
by greenery alone sometimes twisting and almost stopping when
a stick or a rock catches at her clothes and once briefly an arm
lifts as she is held back by a clump of turf

She passes on again with her hips and shoulders parting open the
enfolding fields leaving pools of dark water in her wake and she
comes toward me amid the hiss and crack of leaf and stem
tugged by my breath through the screen of reeds at the head of
my stream and crashes through into this clear water with an
appalling suddenness

Crashes through into this still space where water feels its mass
once more and sky pools around her momentarily while these
forces refocus themselves straining to grip her better and soon
she starts to drift gaining impetus now drifting faster past the
new stone wall and past the place where the willow fell and past
the severed head of a stone Narcissus grinning up at me from the
stream-bed unexpectedly

And passes endlessly beyond the edges of the frame in which I
meant to notice her Oh she was here and again here and here and
here vanishing in the interstices of Is and Was leaving only
afterimages of a garlanded Ophelia with golden hair and a face
made hideous by the rictus of shock and now she has reached the
end of the stretch of stream I have cleared where the weeds and
the reeds thicken up again and the lovely arum lilies close over
her wanting to touch

And Spring passes through, clearing her own passage,
breaking lilies.

## My Time with Biggles

I was with Biggles you know –
never flew, no, not one of the few;
just part of the ground crew.
Not one of the fliers, all goggles and silks and over-to-you;
just one of the lads left down by the hangars
with the waving ladies
and the Polish upper classes.

We'd buff up our boots or blanco the nissens
while Biggles fought Von Someone-or-other for hours
in the peaceful skies over Biggleshill,
or hung round the sun, in wait for the Hun,
hot and alert as a silly-mid-off in the final over-and-out.
When it got colder we'd huddle up to the wireless for warmth,
dizzied with static, startled by crackly outbursts of yelping
from Ginger and Algy whenever they sighted an enemy kite.
And after a kill we would murmur, in Latin, the airman's motto:
Breeding Per Dementia Unto Something Jolly Big, Toodle-pip,
and pat the ladies on the hip
and promise them stockings.

When it was windy we'd go out and watch him dart and crack
about up there like a fly trapped in a miner's hat,
till it was time for him to come down for a pee,
or for tea,
for a pee, or for tea
at the base,
and then I would
rouge the holes in his fuselage
and rosin his ailerons till the damn things sang in the wind . . .
Oh rosin his ailerons, rosin his ailerons, rosin his ailerons . . .
And I'd strop his prop till it cut like a knife.

'SCRAMBLE! SCRAMBLE!'
Biggles always slept fully dressed
but Ginger only slept in his vest
Algy once had to fly in the nude
with bits of a pleasurable interlude
still stuck to his legs
like scrambled eggs

'SCRAMBLE! SCRAMBLE!
Jerry 4,000 angels over Swedenborg!'

out of the sun
watch him come
gun-drunk
grinning Hun
but Biggles spots him
Biggles hums
rumpty-tum
scratches his bum
zooms in
lots of throttle
hot for battle
thumbs the stud
on his slippery stick
and bullets chatter out of him like starlings.
Oh, how the lead hurtles from Biggles' guns!
How his load lightens, how heavy the Hun's.
The Messerschmitt sags, the Iron Cross shatters,
and scalding worms wriggle into frankfurter flesh.
'Donner und Blutwurst!'
One of them wriggles right into his head
the Kraut is dead
should have stayed in bed
the plane goes bang
wizard prang.
'Biggie to base
Biggie's got him
rogered 'im rogered 'im

ring the King
Biggie's done it again!'

Then more of them come from behind a cloud
(a British cloud at that, the swine)
deadly as small boys chucking apple-cores,
and Biggles does his famous roll, his guns tut-tut,
the sky a mass of dotted lines to tear along.

A thousand young pilots drift down
on tapestries woven in Dresden.
They hang like tampons, like shreds
of shag from Biggles' briar.
They litter the landscape like Bombay Duck
on the floor of a curry-shop after a rugby-club dinner.
And Biggles flies amongst them goggles agleam,
leaning out, shouting at them, things like:
'Must dash, poor show, rotten luck,
toodle-pip, toodle-pip!'

Then it's back to the Pantiles,
with the peacocks, trout and fantails,
for cinnamon toast and pale earl grey,
a couple of pipes with a potty vicar
(double trouble, steeple and dottle)
and home to base for a laugh with the lads,
a couple of bottles of viking's-piss,
a heave in the bog,
and an hour or two with a curious mag
in which knickers fight their way off boyish rumps
revealing cricket stumps.

I was with Biggles you know –
never flew, no, not one of the few,
not one of the fliers, all goggles and silks and over-to-you;
just one of the blokes he left behind
with the brave waving ladies and lesser allies.

Who could blame us if we had some fun
while he was up there bashing the Hun?
The ladies were lonely, the ladies were lovely,
superbly bred,
grand in bed,
and the world was ours for hours and hours.
A tickle, a rustle, a fall of silk,
a hint of muscle, a skin like milk.
And Biggles was happy, so what can I say?
With such ladies to lie with, who needs to fly?

Toodle-pip, old man.
Toodle-pip!

# JOHN WHALE

# Face

On a promise of scar tissue I was named
Face, and came to be called Face.
I was made up of spectacular facts.
I invested myself as a flying dog
and waited all year for a dragon.

One day, mad bulls broke the container
and charged the random estate.
There was no clear kingdom to reach.
All through the tropical heatwave
we lived in fear of The Purple Cloud.

I knew one who was crushed:
a lorry buckled the bronze polygon
which couldn't buy his lucky bag;
another fell three hundred feet
out of the summer trip.

One morning, blue globules of ice
littered the metalled field
like the eyes of monstrous frogs.
We smelt for hides and soap in the fog
and came up with nothing.

One night, The Cocky Watchman,
(the one with the moveable hut
and a diet of stale sponge fingers)
stepped outside his valuable railings
and laid a six inch nail in my head.

I knew that expertise in off-ground tick
was no protection for this life.
You needed angel wings
to avoid rumours of The Form,
(known only by their graffiti),

the thought of the hidden hammer,
and reports of that delinquent Guinness,
– the one with the soft blond quiff.
This was my first shared world.
I prepared myself for the next.

# Kynance Cove Again

At Kynance Cove the breakers hit you
slap in the chest, and then again
from sparkling stacks of serpentine.

If you go down to Kynance Cove
time your climb to the cliff's foot.
You really need to watch the tides.

You can come back from Kynance Cove.
There's another way if the tide is in:
past the dead thrift and the dwarf furze.

I'm telling you all this because
I know you've been to Kynance once before,
and you know that it's a sacred place

and because I'm choosing to imagine
that one of these three ravens
croaking and stumbling at the cliff-top

reminds me of my paternal grandfather
whose chest gave way in the fifties,
almost two years before I was born.

## Star Whispers

Our stones screamed across the lake
and we replayed, again and again,
the man who went out across the ice
in silence: a memory to himself.
It was impossible to imagine
the star whispers of his dying breath.

Our stones whistle across the lake
as if the air held wires.
A hunched grey silhouette
is really a starving kingfisher,
and the friend looming out of the fog
has not crossed my mind for months.

## My Crypt Hand

When my heart raced ten and a half miles
from Shibden up to Blackstone Edge
my words flew faster than the mail,
too fast, I know, I spoke too fast
like one I've met with in a dream
your look of shame went through my speech
and I felt an iceberg on my breast.
When you moved into marriage
I would not stop it for the world,
having no world to give in return.
I was not born to live alone:
I said *I've a pain in my knees, M,*
*a pain in my knees*, knowing how to please,
loving you softly, gentleman-like.

You little ween this ink shed of my pen:
I will not give you heart's-ease,
sweet allison, Venus's looking-glass
or even the dwarf passion-flower
to make up your northern nosegay.
These words keep myself from myself,
they oil the soft cog of my heart
which I've washed, again and again,
in corrosive sublimate.
Think only of Fontainebleau grapes
and clean Normandy pears
as my body rumbles back to Halifax
from Terfliz in the dusty Caucasus.
I give you this, my crypt hand.

NOTE    *Anne Lister (1791–1840) lived at Shibden Hall,*
*Halifax and was the author of numerous diaries which*
*chronicle her romantic and sexual relationships with other*
*women. Some of the diaries are in a coded cipher which she*
*refers to as her 'crypt hand'.*

## Galileo's Watch

It moves! It moves!
His gloved hand tracks across
the empty continent of paper
at the rate of glaciers
cutting schists to alps
up in the Valtellina.

Out here the possessive apostrophe
is only a drop in the ocean.
Even the indigo sworl from his nib,
which resembles a question-mark
as much as the cold Peruvian current
licking the kink in the Andes,
must, like the worst depression,
obey the corkscrew laws of hemispheres.

In my Vallombrosan childhood
the leaves fell as fast as feathers,
the two clocks ticked different times
as I watched them swing, this way and that,
and the leaves fell with regularity
through my Vallombrosan childhood.

As I wait for this jewelled hand,
the Horn of Africa slides towards Arabia,
narrowing the Red Sea by just one inch
in a Biblical lifetime.
I've watched its minute progress now
for almost three hundred and
fifty nine years – and I'm sure:
It moves! It moves!

NOTE    *In November 1992 the Pope signed the last document
in the long, drawn-out process of 'rehabilitating' Galileo.*

# 1790s Diary

At 2 oclock this Afternoon I buried Poor Lydia Betts.
I did not know she was ill, until she was Dead.
Snip, Fly and Spring cornered and Killed a fine Hare
out on the far Pasture. She tasted well!
By the Papers a very great Rebellion in France.
Veal Collops, Calfs Fry and a boiled Bullock's Heart.

So bitter cold! I had my worn Bay-Mare,
old Peggy, shot before I came downstairs.
I had her Skinned as I intend to have her tanned.
It was an Act of Charity to do as I have done.
A Juicy Tench, Pigeon Pye and a Hashed Calfs Head.

Young Fly ran off with Betty Cary's Mutton
undressed, and eat it all up. A Great Commotion.
I had the Hound hanged this Evening.
The News is the King and Queen of France
carried back to Paris, and on Lloyd's Paper.
Veal rosted, Stewed Eels, two Fellfares and a Blackbird.

My Eye healed. Thank God! I did it by the Tail
of my black Tom Cat. Dreadful times ahead.
The cruel Blood-Thirsty French have killed their King.
God save the Queen, 2 children and their Aunt.
Piggs Face, Green Goose and Giblet Soup.

# The Invertebrate Zenith

*O for a life of sensations . . .*

In the soft name of science
this is the place for poetry.
At the invertebrate zenith
shaming the arid cameleon
with the most unpoetical
of all God's creatures,
this one fine specimen of
the *octopus dofleini*.

It has no rigid form, no
back-boned articulation –
just three pumping hearts
and the most talented epidermis
known to man, and a second
'touch memory' which isn't.
Fantastic elastic cephalopoda
you can crawl, walk or swim,
and your chromatophores command
immediate volcanic change.
Your lost limbs return like phantoms
and like phantoms change their form
to suit the various functions
of the three short years to
all-out molluscan surge.

You are not part of this screening
and we have no anaesthetic.
You convulse with scarlet pain
at the touch of this philosophy.
Your bubbling tears dissolve
under the poet's ruthless lens.
My bleached linen cuffs
are like blotting paper.
Piss your unprintable ink.

# Waterloo Teeth

After Soult and Ney and the Imperial Guard
had gone down among the rotting corn,
we fell upon the rain-soaked bodies of the dead
and ripped lace gorgettes from the dandy officers.
From the rosy cheeks of English plough-boys
we pulled two hundred sets of perfect teeth.

Chalky moonlight kisses the domed pavilion
and turns the Sussex stone to ivory.
Inside, the giddy lovers lose themselves
in chiaroscuro and entangled chinoiserie.
Their tongues explore the sea-horse, walrus
and hippopotamus which grips their foreign teeth.

I conquered all Europe with my attitudes:
Daphne, Miranda, Sibyl, Bacchante.
I sent men's names through the world's loud mouth.
But when I was only poor young Emma Hart,
I took my self to pawn, again and again,
rather than sell my unbroken lines of delicate teeth.

Please don't make your Waterloo eyes at me –
as if there's a world beyond the moon.
All day I dream of Freddy drenched in Flanders.
So when you ask me again how old I am,
I'll purse my lips and make these words your rhyme:
*the same age as my tongue, a little older than my teeth.*

# Salt Fish (Stories)

### I

All Saturday night the salt fish
leaked its brine into the soaking-pan
and the arched fillet gave off
minute flecks of slow-dissolving flesh.
Its bulk rises silently to a phantom life.
By Sunday morning what was once
faceless, straw-coloured stiff
flops in a rich scum on the ring.
Served new risen with the bacon fat,
buttercup flesh in perfect shields.

### II

Nosing the current off Newfoundland
the large-eyed, whiskery cod-head
fingers the edge of the continental shelf,
its missing flanks sliced, dried and casked.

### III

Trace the black lines down
through the geometric sixties
zig-zag on the formica table-top
to cross-overs, collisions and
the darker triangular dead-ends,
the trails of muddled heroes
caught in a strange breakfast
of war and comics, and comic homely war,
a warm emulsion of fish
lubricating the harsh tang of salt.

One great athletic uncle who
raced Buffalo Bill on foot and won.
'And him on a horse as well!'
Incapable of following Rorkes Drift
in *The Hotspur*'s wordy anniversaries,
*The Hurricane*'s 'Gott im Himmel!
Banzai! Banzai! Zeros at 12 o'clock!'
the ex-boss with a stomach full of glass,
Szenna's heroic crawl across the icy Baltic
or poor young Hughie lost at Anzio.

The budgie rattles in the Anderson
with grans, aunts, uncles, dogs and cats.
The sheer extravagance of oranges.
A mouth soused in deep Atlantic.

# Unknown Regions

*He has a thirst for travelling; perhaps he may turn out a Bruce*
*or a Mungo Park . . . he said he should prefer not to know*
*the sources of the Nile, and that there should be some unknown*
*regions preserved as hunting-grounds for the poetic imagination.*
     – GEORGE ELIOT, *Middlemarch*


I   *Source of the Nile*

Irritable curiosity drove him to it.
Across the blinding Nubian desert
he kept his eyes fixed on the stars
and saw a horde of Saharan Visigoths

flying before the first simoom,
met the tribe who fed exclusively on lion
and ate beef sliced from the live flank.
The laird was drugged on Ethiopian bream.

If the third cataract left him speechless,
the Nile's source brought him to his knees.
Jupiter stood above the mountains of Geesh
and the quicksilver rose twenty two inches.

*But grief rolled upon me like a torrent.*
Attacked by a clear case of the horrors
he made oat-cakes out of wild grasses
and bathed himself in the streams of Clyde.

From the confusion of Abyssinian tongues
and the din of bloody courtly battles
he recalled the princess Ozoro Esther
screaming in the metropolis of Gondar.

In his inaudible dreams the roar of waters
drowned the workmen forging his obelisk,
his name adrift in a sea of hieroglyphs
above the Carron's newest smelting-plant.


II    *The Eye of Providence*

Nearly five hundred miles
from the nearest settlement,
robbed, stripped and
surrounded by lions

my eye was irresistibly caught
by the beauty of a small moss,
its delicate conformation
of roots, leaves and capsula.

# Brioche

*Qu'ils mangent de la brioche.*
— ATTRIBUTED TO MARIE ANTOINETTE

She lay beneath the stomach of the king.
A slight rustle inside her. Then nothing.
He charged through his beloved Fontainebleau,
a trail of broken bracken in his wake.

She turned herself over and tried hard to sleep,
to dream of an island crowned with poplars
and breakfast surrounded by ribboned cows,
the deep orange yolks of her darling hens.

She flexed her tense feet down in the sheets
and her toe-nails seemed strangely sharp,
her downy shins felt scaly and rough.
Her shoulders sprouted little leathery wings,

a barb and tail curled out from her behind
and her claws walked off to play with the dauphin.
She felt the stones in her necklace tighten
as they promised to fricassee her liver.

When she struggled hard to say nothing
they forced the common little word brioche
out of her harpy mouth and showered the crowds
with the crumbs of the blood they wanted.

# The Nondescript

And so he went in search of curare,
wourali, woorara, urali, unrari,
losing himself among the complex
arteries of the mangroves and lianas
where he learnt the habits of ant-eaters,
the reverse gait of the three-toed-sloth,
and the gentlemanly art of travel
on a twelve foot grinning cayman.
From the Macushi and the Ancoway
he found how one small spike
could make a large dog slide into death
while still barking at strangers.

Twice he queued hours for a glimpse
of the blood of St Januarius
liquefying in the heat of Naples,
and with the same fascination
had mice, rabbits, cats and dogs
and a host of obliging asses
slide casually from life to death.
Poor Jenny, the first gorilla
ever to die in Warrington,
was cured and then set up
(with ass's ears) as Martin Luther.
Nothing was ever simply stuffed.

Old miners swore blind they'd
seen birds of paradise stalking
the wooded outskirts of Wakefield.
But Walton Hall was so fully blown
that there was nothing left in it.
Tame herons were shot upon their nests,
hounds tore through the smiling game,
and fire consumed his scribbled notes.
He left behind 'The Nondescript'

or wild man of noble countenance,
which good scientific opinion identifies
as the very arsehole of a howler.

# Notes on Contributors

SEAN BOUSTEAD was born in 1969. He studied English and European Modern Literature at the University of Essex and now lives in Cheshire. He edits the poetry magazine *Walking Naked* and enjoys fell-walking. Like many recent graduates, he has worked at a number of occupations from teacher to pizza chef and now hopes to pursue a career in accountancy. His poems have been published in *Envoi* and in *Agenda*, as well as in *Walking Naked*.

COLETTE BRYCE was born in 1970 in Northern Ireland. She lives in London and works as a bookseller.

KATE CLANCHY was born in Glasgow in 1965 and educated at Exeter College, Oxford. She lives in London and works as a teacher and freelance journalist. Her short story *Boom* was awarded a prize in the 1993 London Arts Board competition. The poem *Men* was specially commended in the 1994 Arvon International Poetry Competition. She received an Eric Gregory Award in 1994. Some of the poems in this anthology first appeared in *The Sunday Times*, *The Independent*, *The Scotsman*, *The Times Educational Supplement*, *Ambit* and *Rialto*.

OLIVER COMINS was born in Warwickshire in 1957 and grew up in the town of Kenilworth. He was educated at the University of York, and began working with personal computers in the Midlands in the early 1980s, while his spare time was occupied with poetry and cricket. He now lives in Oxfordshire with his wife Christine and baby son Oliver and works in the computer industry. His poetry has appeared in a wide variety of magazines, including *Argo*, *Smiths Knoll* and *The Honest Ulsterman*. In 1992 the Mandeville Press published the pamphlet *Playing out Time in an Awkward Light*.

CHRISTINA DUNHILL is Writer in Residence at Cookham Wood Women's Prison. She teaches creative writing at the City Literary Institute in London and in private workshops. She was a finalist in the 1993/4 Arvon Poetry Competition and has also won prizes in the Bridport, the South West and the Kitson Trust competitions. She has edited an anthology of women's poetry, *As Girls Could Boast* (Oscars Press, 1994). Her poems have appeared in *The Observer*, *Verse*, *The North*, *Rialto*, *Tampa Review*, *Poetry London Newsletter* and several anthologies including *Jugular Defences*, an AIDS anthology (Oscars Press, 1994). Her stories are featured in *Sleeping Rough* (Lime Tree, 1991) and *Wild Hearts* (Sheba, 1991).

ALICE OSWALD was born in 1966 and studied Classics at New College, Oxford. She trained as a professional gardener at RHS Wisley and lives and works in Devon. Her poems have been published in *Planet*, *London Magazine*, *The Forward Anthology* and *The Spectator*. In 1994 she received an Eric Gregory Award.

RICHARD PRICE was born in 1966 in Scotland. He studied journalism, followed by English and librarianship at the University of Strathclyde. He was awarded a doctorate in 1994 for his study of the Scottish novelist Neil M. Gunn. He has edited various literary magazines, including *Gairfish*, *Verse* and *Southfields*. He is co-founder of Vennel Press which specializes in new Scottish poetry. He has been published in *Northwords*, *New Writing Scotland*, *Oxford Poetry* and in Daniel O'Rourke's *Dream State: The New Scottish Poetry* (Polygon, 1994). He works as a curator at the British Library in London.

MIKE VENNER was born in 1944 and educated at Oxford. He has lived in Peru and Spain as well as Britain, while working variously as a teacher, writer, builder, actor and playing in several folk and rock bands. He now lives in Bristol. He is a frequent performer of his poetry, often with other musicians. His poems have been published in *South West Review* and *Wayzgoose*.

JOHN WHALE was born in Liverpool in 1956. He now lives in Leeds where he teaches at the University. He has published in a variety of magazines including *Stand* and *Versus* and was a prize winner in the 1992 National Poetry Competition.

# Acknowledgements

SEAN BOUSTEAD: 'Advice' and 'A Landscape After War' in *Walking Naked*; 'Bob Turner and His Wife' in *Envoi*; 'Young Mothers' in *Agenda*.

COLETTE BRYCE: 'Woman & Turkey' in *Smiths Knoll*.

KATE CLANCHY: 'Men' in *The Independent* and the *Arvon/Observer 1994* anthology; 'The Aerialist' in *The Scotsman*; 'Can't Argue With It' and 'Timetable' in *Times Educational Supplement*; 'Slattern' in *The Sunday Times*; 'Designs' in *Ambit*; 'Pathetic Fallacy' in *Rialto*.

OLIVER COMINS: 'Quarry' in *Argo*; 'Bar Staff' and 'Playing Out Time in an Awkward Light I, II & III' in *Giant Steps*; 'The Coral Club' in *The Honest Ulsterman*; 'Rural' in *Odyssey*; 'Beside the Seaside' in *Other Poetry*; 'Floral Clock' in *Smiths Knoll*; 'Light Relief' in *Wallingford Magazine*. Some of these poems are also included in a pamphlet called *Playing Out Time in an Awkward Light* published by the Mandeville Press in 1992.

CHRISTINA DUNHILL: 'Old People' in *The Observer Arvon Poetry Collection 1993*; 'White Wolf' in *The South West Poetry Anthology 1994*; 'Ring of Kerry' in *Language of Water, Language of Fire* (Oscars Press, 1992); 'Owltime' in *Rialto*; 'To One of Her Sisters' in *Tampa Review, Poetry London Newsletter*; 'The Darts' in *Verse*; 'Denise Delieu' in *The Bridport Prize* anthology, 1993, and *Riding Pillion* (Poetry Business Anthology, 1994); 'Say "Moose" for Me' in *As Girls Could Boast* (Oscars Press, 1994) and *The Margot Jane Memorial Prize* pamphlet, 1994.

ALICE OSWALD: 'A Greyhound in the Evening After a Long Day of Rain', 'Pruning in Frost', 'The Glass House', 'When a Stone Was Wrecking His Country', 'A Wood Coming into Leaf' and 'My Neighbour, Mrs Kersey' in *Planet*; 'Sleep' and 'Sonnet' in *London Magazine*; 'The Melon Grower' in *New Statesman*.

RICHARD PRICE: 'Saying the swim' in *Interference*; 'With is' in *Verse*; 'Block' in *Contraflow on the Super Highway* (Southfields, 1994); 'Sense and a minor fever' and 'A new establishment' in *Sense and a Minor Fever* (Vennel, 1993); 'Stopper' in *Northwords*; 'Tie-breaker' in *Casablanca*.

MIKE VENNER: 'When My Ship Comes In' in *South West Review*; 'A Sense of Place' in *Wayzgoose*.

JOHN WHALE: 'Star Whispers' in *Versus*; '1790s Diary' in *Stand*; 'Salt Fish (Stories)' in *The Tempest*; 'The Nondescript' in the Poetry Society's *1992 National Poetry Competition Prize Winners* anthology.

*New and Recent Poetry from Anvil*

**HEATHER BUCK**
*Psyche Unbound*

**TONY CONNOR**
*Metamorphic Adventures*

**HARRY GUEST**
*Coming to Terms*

**MICHAEL HAMBURGER**
*Collected Poems 1941–1994*

**JAMES HARPUR**
*A Vision of Comets*

**ANTHONY HOWELL**
*First Time in Japan*

**MARIUS KOCIEJOWSKI**
*Doctor Honoris Causa*

**PETER LEVI**
*The Rags of Time*

**CHARLES MADGE**
*Of Love, Time and Places*
SELECTED POEMS

**DENNIS O'DRISCOLL**
*Long Story Short*

**PHILIP SHERRARD**
*In the Sign of the Rainbow*
SELECTED POEMS 1940–1989

**RUTH SILCOCK**
*A Wonderful View of the Sea*

**SUE STEWART**
*Inventing the Fishes*

A catalogue of our publications is available on request

## By Carol Ann Duffy

### STANDING FEMALE NUDE

' ... a book that marks the debut of a genuine and original poet.'

– ROBERT NYE in *The Times*

'Carol Ann Duffy is a very pure poet ... It is good to see a crusading sensibility refusing to surrender any touch of art to the urgency of its cause.'

– PETER PORTER in *The Observer*

### SELLING MANHATTAN

' ... not only a fresh voice but a dexterity with language, that glorious juggling which poets sometimes achieve with a sense of surprise even to themselves.'

– ELIZABETH JENNINGS in *The Independent*

### THE OTHER COUNTRY

'*The Other Country* is a slim volume like few that have been published recently: urgent, packed with future classics – a book that proclaims that poetry is alive.'

– PETER FORBES in *The Guardian*

'It voices political-erotic challenge, always knows where it's going, and has serious fun on the way.'

– RUTH PADEL in the *TLS*

### MEAN TIME

'Carol Ann Duffy is one of the freshest and bravest talents to emerge in British poetry – any poetry – for years.'

– EAVAN BOLAND in *The Independent on Sunday*

'*Mean Time* ... maintains the standards of its predecessors, and may, in fact, surpass them in its treatment of love and memory ... to have something to add on these matters, and to deliver it with such force and economy, indicates gifts of a high order.'

– SEAN O'BRIEN in *The Sunday Times*

*Mean Time* received the Forward Poetry Prize and the Whitbread Poetry Award for 1993.